QUIET TALKS ON PRAYER

S. D. GORDON

Marshall Pickering

Also available by the same author
The Healing Christ

Pickering and Inglis
Marshall Pickering
3 Beggarwood Lane, Basingstoke, Hants RG23 7LP, UK

Copyright © 1984 by The Christian Library
Originally published in 1904
This edition first published in the UK in 1986 by Pickering
and Inglis Ltd
Part of the Marshall Pickering Holdings Group
A subsidiary of the Zondervan Corporation

British Library CIP Data

Gordon, S.D.
Quiet talks on prayer.
1. Prayer
I. Title
248.3'2   BV215

ISBN 0-7208-0694-1

Printed and bound in Great Britain by Anchor Brendon Ltd,
Tiptree, Essex

CONTENTS

I. THE MEANING AND MISSION OF PRAYER

The Greatest Outlet of Power

Five Outlets of Power.

A great sorrow has come into the heart of God. Let it be told only in hushed voice—one of His worlds is *a prodigal!* Hush your voice yet more—*ours* is that prodigal world. Let your voice soften down still more—*we* have *consented* to the prodigal part of the story. But, in softest tones yet, He has won some of us back with His strong tender love. And now let the voice ring out with great gladness—we won ones may be the pathway back to God for the others. That is His earnest desire. That should be our dominant ambition. For that purpose He has endowed us with peculiar power.

There is one inlet of power in the life—anybody's life—any kind of power: just one inlet—the Holy Spirit. He is power. He is in every one who opens his door to God. He eargerly enters every open door. He comes in by our invitation and consent. His presence within is the vital thing.

But with many of us while He is in, He is not in control: in as guest; not as host. That is to say He is hindered in His natural movements; tied up, so that He cannot do what He would. And so we are not conscious or only partially conscious of His presence. And others are still less so. But to yield to His mastery, to cultivate His friendship, to give Him full swing—that will result in what is called power. One inlet of power—the Holy Spirit in control.

There are five outlets of power: five avenues through which this One within shows Himself, and revels His power.

First: through the life, what we are. Just simply what we are. If we be right the power of God will be constantly flowing out, though we be not conscious of it. It throws the keenest kind of emphasis on a man being right in his life. There will be an eager desire to serve. Yet we may constantly do more in what we are than in what we do. We may serve better in the lives we live than in the best service we ever give. The memory of that should bring rest to your spirit when a bit tired, and may be disheartened because tired.

Second: through the lips, what we say. It may be said stammeringly and falteringly. But if said your best with the desire to please the Master it will be God-blest. I have heard a man talk. And he stuttered and blushed and got his grammar badly tangled, but my heart burned as I listened. And I have heard a man talk with smooth speech, and it rolled off me as easily as it rolled out of him. Do your best, and leave the rest. If we are in touch with God His fire burns whether the tongue stammer or has good control of its powers.

Third: through our service, what we do. It may be done bunglingly and blunderingly. Your best may not be the best, but if it be your best it will bring a harvest.

Fourth: through our money, what we do not keep, but loosen out for God. Money comes the nearest to omnipotence of anything we handle.

And, fifth: through our prayer, what we claim in Jesus' name.

And by all odds the greatest of these is the outlet through prayer. The power of a life touches just one spot, but the touch is tremendous. What is there we think to be compared with a pure, unselfish, gently strong life. Yet its power is limited to one spot where it is being lived. Power through the lips depends wholly upon the life back of the lips. Words that come brokenly are often made burning and eloquent by the life behind them. And words that are smooth and easy, often have all their meaning sapped by the life back of them. Power through service may be great, and may be touching many spots, yet it is always less than that of a life. Power through money depends wholly upon the motive back of the money. Begrudged money, stained money, soils the treasury. That which comes nearest to omnipotence also comes nearest to impotence. But the power loosened out through prayer is as tremendous, at the least, to say no more just now, is as tremendous as the power of a true fragrant life and, mark you, *and,* may touch not one spot but wherever in the whole round world you may choose to turn it.

The greatest thing any one can do for God and for man is to pray. It is not the only thing. But it is the chief thing. A correct balancing of the possible powers one may exert puts it first. For if a man is to pray right, he must first *be* right in his motives and life. And if a man *be* right, and put the practice of praying in its right place, then his serving and giving and speaking will be fairly fragrant with the presence of God.

The great people of the earth to-day are the people who pray. I do not mean those who talk about prayer; nor those who say they believe in prayer; nor yet those who can explain about prayer; but I mean these people who *take* time and *pray.* They have not time. It must be taken from something else. This something else is important. Very important, and pressing, but still less important and less pressing than prayer. There are people that put prayer first, and group the other items in life's schedule around and after prayer.

There are the people to-day who are doing the most for God; in winning souls; in solving problems; in awakening churches; in supplying both men and money for mission posts; in keeping fresh and strong lives far off in sacrificial service on the foreign field where the thickest fighting is going on; in keeping the old earth sweet awhile longer.

It is wholly a secret service. We do not know who these people are, though sometimes shrewd guesses may be made. I often think that sometimes we pass some plain-looking woman quietly slipping out of church; gown been turned two or three times; bonnet fixed over more than once; hands that have not known much of the softening of gloves; and we hardly give her a passing thought, and do not know, nor guess, that perhaps *she* is the one who is doing far more for her church, and for the world, and for God than a hundred who would claim more attention and thought, *because she prays;* truly prays as the Spirit of God inspires and guides.

Let me put it this way: God will do as a result of the praying of the humblest one here what otherwise He *would* not
do. Yes, I can make it stronger than that, and I must make it
stronger, for the Book does. Listen: God will do in answer to
the prayer of the weakest one here what otherwise He *could*
not do. "Oh!" someone thinks, "you are getting that too
strong now." Well, you listen to Jesus' own words in that last
long quiet talk He had with the eleven men between the upper
room and the olive-grove. John preserves much of that talk
for us. Listen: "Ye did not choose Me, but I chose you, and
appointed you, that ye should go and bear fruit, and that
your fruit should abide: that"—listen, a part of the purpose
why we have been chosen—"that whatsoever ye shall ask of
the Father in My name, He *may* give it you."[1] Mark that
word "may"; not "shall" this time but *may*. "Shall" throws
the matter over on God—His purpose. "May" throws it over
upon us—our cooperation. That is to say our praying makes
it possible for God to do what otherwise He could not do.

And if you think into it a bit, this fits in with the true conception of prayer. In its simplest analysis prayer—all prayer
—has, must have, two parts. First, a God to give. "Yes," you
say, "certainly, a God wealthy, willing, all of that." And,
just as certainly, there must be a second factor, *a man to
receive*. Man's willingness is God's channel to the earth. God
never crowds nor coerces. Everything God does for man and
through man He does with man's consent, always. With due
reverence, but very plainly, let it be said that God can do
nothing for the man with shut hand and shut life. There must
be an open hand and heart and life *through* which God can
give what He longs to. An open life, an open hand, open upward, is the pipe line of communication between the heart of
God and this poor befooled old world. Our prayer is God's
opportunity to get into the world that would shut Him out.

[1] John 15:16

In touch with a planet.

Prayer opens a whole planet to a man's activities. I can as really be touching hearts for God in far away India or China through prayer, as though I were there. Not in as many ways as though there, but as truly. Understand me, I think the highest possible *privilege* of service is in those far off lands. There the need is greatest, the darkness densest, and the pleading call most eloquently pathetic. And if one *may* go there—happy man!—if one be *privileged* to go to the honoured place of service he may then use all five outlets direct in the spot where he is.

Yet this is only one spot. But his relationship is as wide as his Master's and his sympathies should be. A man may be in Africa, but if his heart be in touch with Jesus it will be burning for *a world*. Prayer puts us into direct dynamic touch with a world.

A man may go aside to-day, and shut his door, and as really spend a half-hour in India—I am thinking of my words as I say them, it seems so much to say, and yet it is true—as really spend a half hour of his life in India for God as though he were there in person. *Is* that true? If it be true, surely you and I must get more half-hours for this secret service. Without any doubt he may turn his key and be for a bit of time as potentially in China by the power of prayer, as though there in actual bodily form. I say *potentially* present. Of course not consciously present. But in the *power exerted upon men* he may be truly present at the objective point of his prayer. He may give a new meaning to the printed page being read by some native down in Africa. He may give a new tongue of flame to the preacher or teacher. He may make it easier for men to accept the story of Jesus, and then to yield themselves to Jesus—yonder men swept and swayed by evil spirits, and by prejudices for generations—make it easier for them to accept the story, and, if need be, to cut with loved ones, and step out and up into a new life.

Some earnest heart enters an objection here, perhaps. You are thinking that if you were there you could influence men by your personal contact, by the living voice. So you could. And there must be the personal touch. Would that there were many times more going for that blessed personal touch. But this is the thing to mark keenly both for those who may go, and for those who must stay: no matter where you are you do more through your praying than through your personality. If you were in India you could *add your personality to your prayer.* That would be a great thing to do. But whether there or here, you must first win the victory, every step, every life, every foot of the way, in secret, in the spirit-realm, and then add the mighty touch of your personality in service. You can do *more* than pray, *after* you have prayed. But you can *not* do more than pray *until* you have prayed. And just there is where we all seemed to make a slip at times, and many of us are yet making it—a bad slip. We think we can do more where we are through our service: then prayer to give power to service. *No*—with the blackest underscoring of emphasis, let it be said—NO. We can do no thing of real power until we have done the prayer thing.

Here is a man by my side. I can talk to him. I can bring my personality to bear upon him, that I may win him. But before I can influence his will a jot for God, I must first have won the victory in the secret place. Intercession is winning the victory over the chief, and service is taking the field after the chief is driven off. Such service is limited by the limitation of personality to one place. This spirit-telegraphy called prayer puts a man into direct dynamic touch with a planet.

There are some of our friends who think themselves of the practical sort who say, "the great thing is work: prayer is good, and right, but the great need is to be doing something practical." The truth is that when one understands about prayer, and puts prayer in its right place in his life, he finds a new motive power burning in his bones to be *doing;* and further he finds that it is the doing that grows out of praying that is mightiest in touching human hearts. And he finds further yet with a great joy that he may be *doing* something for an entire world. His service becomes as broad as his Master's thought.

Intercession is Service.

It helps greatly to remember that intercession is service: the chief service of a life on God's plan. It is unlike all other forms of service, and superior to them in this: that it has fewer limitations. In all other service we are constantly limited by space, bodily strength, equipment, material obstacles, difficulties involved in the peculiar differences of personality. Prayer knows no such limitations. It ignores space. It may be free of expenditure of bodily strength, where rightly practiced, and one's powers are under proper control. It goes directly, by the telegraphy of spirit, into men's hearts, quietly passes through walls, and past locks unhindered, and comes into most direct touch with the inner heart and will to be affected.

In service, as ordinarily understood, one is limited to the space where his body is, the distance his voice can reach, the length of time he can keep going before he must quit to eat, or rest, or sleep. He is limited by walls, and locks, by the prejudices of men's minds, and by those peculiar differences of temperament which must be studied in laying siege to men's hearts.

The whole circle of endeavour in winning men includes such an infinite variety. There is speaking the truth to a number of persons, and to one at a time; the doing of needed kindly acts of helpfulness, supplying food, and the like; there is teaching; the almost omnipotent ministry of money; the constant contact with a pure unselfish life; letter writing; printer's ink in endless variety. All these are in God's plan for winning men. But the intensely fascinating fact to mark is this:—that the real victory in all of this service is won in secret, beforehand, by prayer, and these other indispensable things are the moving upon the works of the enemy, and claiming the victory already won. And when these things are put in their proper order, prayer first, and the other things second; *second*, I say, not omitted, not slurred over; done with all the earnestness and power of brain and hand and heart possible; but done *after* the victory has been won in secret, against the real foe, and done *while* the winner is still claiming the victory already assured,—then will come far greater achievements in this outer open service.

Then we go into this service with that fine spirit of expectancy that sweeps the field at the start, and steadily sticks on the stubbornly contested spots until the whipped foe turns tail, and goes. Prayer is striking the winning blow at the concealed enemy. Service is gathering up the results of that blow among the men we see and touch. Great patience and tact and persistence are needed in the service because each man must be influenced in his own will. But the shrewd strategy that wins puts the keen stiff secret fighting first.

The Spirit Switchboard.

Electricity is a strange element. It is catalogued in the study of physics. It is supposed to be properly classed among the forces of nature. Yet it seems to have many properties of the spirit world. Those who know most of it say they know least of what it is. Some of the laws of its being have been learned, and so its marvellous power harnessed for man's use, but in much ignorance of what it is. It seems almost to belong somewhere in between the physical and spirit realms. It furnishes many smiles of graphic helpfulness in understanding more nearly much truth of the Spirit life.

In the power-house where the electricity is being wooed into man's harnessing, or generated, as the experts say, is found a switchboard, or switch-room with a number of boards. Here in a large city plan a man may go and turn a switch, that is, move a little handle, a very short distance. It is a very simple act, easily performed, involving almost no strength. But that act has loosened the power in the house back of the switchboard out along the wires, and perhaps lighted a whole section of the city. He goes in again at another hour, and turns *this* set of switches, and *this,* and sets in motion maybe scores of cars, carying swiftly, hundreds of passengers. Again he goes in, and moves the little handles and sets in motion the wheels in some factory employing hundreds of operatives.

It is a secret service, usually as far as any observers are concerned. It is a very quiet, matter of fact service. But the power influenced is unmeasured and immeasurable. And no one, seemingly, thus far, can explain the mysterious but tremendous agent involved. Does the fluid—*is* it a fluid? or, what?— pass *through* the wire? or, *around* the wire? The experts say they do not know. But the laws which it obeys are known. And as men comply with them its almost omnipotence is manifested.

Just such a switch-room in the spirit realm is one's prayer-room. Every one who will may have such a spirit switching-board in his life. There he may go and in compliance with the laws of the power used loosen out the gracious persuasive irresistible power of God *where he wills to;* now in Japan; now in China; among the hungry human hearts of India's plains and mountains; again in Africa which is full as near to where Jesus sits as is England or America; and now into the house across the alley from your home; and down in the slum district; and now into your preacher's heart for next Sunday's work; and now again unto the hearts of those you will be meeting in the settlement house, or the mission school.

Children are not allowed at the electrical switchboard, nor any unskilled hand. For misuse means possibility of great damage to property and life. And the spirit switchboard does not yield to the unskilled touch. Though sometimes there seems to be much tampering by those with crude fingers, and with selfish desire to turn this current to personal advantage merely.

It takes skill here. Yet such is our winsome God's wondrous plan that skill may come to any one who is willing; simply that—who is willing; and it comes *very simply* too.

Strange too, as with the electrical counterpart, the thing is beyond full or satisfying explanation.

How does it come to pass that a man turns a few handles, and miles away great wheels begin to revolve, and enormous power is manifested? Will some one kindly explain? Yet we know it is so, and men govern their actions by that knowledge.

How does it come to pass that a woman in Iowa prays for the conversion of her skeptical husband, and he, down in the thick of the most absorbing congress Washington has known since the civil war, and in full ignorance of her purpose becomes conscious and repeatedly conscious of the presence and power of the God in whose existence he does not believe; and months afterwards with his keen, legally trained mind, finds the calendar to fit together the beginning of her praying with the beginning of his unwelcome consciousness? Will some one kindly explain? Ah! who can, adequately! Yet the facts, easy ascertainable, are there, and evidenced in the complete change in the life and calling of the man.

How comes it to pass that a woman in Missouri praying for a friend of keen intellectual skepticality in Glasgow, who can skillfully measure and parry argument, yet finds afterwards that the time of her praying is the time of his, at first decidedly unwelcome, but finally radical change of convictions! Yet groups of thoughtful men and women know these two instances to be even so though unable to explain how.

And as the mysterious electrical power is being used by obedience to its laws, even so is the power of praying being used by many who understand simply enough of its laws to obey, and to bring the stupendous results.

The Broad Inner Horizon.

This suggests at once that the rightly rounded Christian life has two sides; the *out*-side, and the *inner* side. To most of us the outer side seems the greater. The living, the serving, the giving, the doing, the absorption in life's work, the contact with men, with the great majority the sheer struggle for existence—these take the greater thought and time of us all. They seem to be the great business of life even to those of us who thoroughly believe in the inner life.

But when the real eyes open, the inner eyes that see the unseen, the change of perspective is first ludicrous, then terrific, then pathetic. Ludicrous, because of the change of proportions; terrific, because of the issues at stake; pathetic, because of strong men that see not, and push on spending splendid strength whittling stocks. The outer side is narrow in its limits. It has to do with food and clothing, bricks and lumber, time and the passing hour, the culture of the mind, the joys of social contact, the smoothing of the way for the suffering. And it needs not to be said, that these are right; they belong in the picture; they are its physical background.

The inner side *includes all of these,* and stretches infinitely beyond. Its limits are broad; broad as the home of man; with its enswathing atmosphere added. It touches the inner spirit. It moves in upon the motives, the loves, the heart. It moves out upon the myriad spirit-beings and forces that swarm ceaselessly about the earth staining and sliming men's souls and lives. It moves up to the arm of God in cooperation with His great love-plan for a world.

Shall we follow for a day one who has gotten the true perspective? Here is the outer side: a humble home, a narrow circle, tending the baby, patching, sewing, cooking, calling; *or,* measuring dry goods, chopping a typewriter, checking up a ledger, feeding the swift machinery, endless stitching, gripping a locomotive lever, pushing the plow, tending the stock, doing the chores, tiresome examination papers; and all the rest of the endless, endless, doing, day by day, of the commonplace treadmill things, that must be done, that fill out the day of the great majority of human lives. This one whom we are following unseen is doing quietly, cheerily his daily round, with a bit of sunshine in his face, a light in his eye, and lightness in his step, and the commonplace place becomes uncommon by reason of the presence of this man with the uncommon spirit. He is working for God. No, better, he is working with God. He has an unseen Friend at his side. That changes all. The common drudgery ceases to be common, and ceases to be drudgery because it is done for such an uncommon Master. That is the outer, the narrow side of this life: not narrow in itself but in its proportion to the whole.

Now, hold your breath, and look, for here is the inner side where the larger work of life is being done. Here is the quiet bit of time alone with God, with the Book. The door is shut, as the Master said. Now it is the morning hour with a bit of made light, for the sun is busy yet farther east. Now it is the evening hour, with the sun speeding towards western service, and the bed invitingly near. There is a looking up into God's face; then keen but reverent reading, and then a simple intelligent pleading with its many variations of this—"Thy will be done, in the Victor's name." God Himself is here, in this inner room. The angels are here. This room opens out into and is in direct touch with a spirit space as wide as the earth. The horizon of this room is as broad as the globe. God's presence with this man makes it so.

To-day a half hour is spent in China, for its missionaries, its native Christians, its millions, the printed page, the personal contact, the telling of the story, the school, the dispensary, the hospital. And in through the petitions runs this golden thread—"Victory in Jesus' name: victory in Jesus' name; to-day: to-day: Thy will be being done: the other will undone: victory in Jesus' name." To-morrow's bit of time is largely spent in India perhaps. And so this man with the narrow outer horizon and the broad inner horizon pushes his spirit-way through Japan, India, Ceylon, Persia, Arabia, Turkey, Africa, Europe's papal lands, the South American States, the home land, its cities, frontiers, slums, the home town, the home church, the man across the alley; in and out; out and in; the tide of prayer sweeps quietly, resistlessly day by day.

This is the true Christian life. This man is winning souls and refreshing lives in these far-off lands and in near-by places as truly as though he were in each place. This is the Master's plan. The true follower of Jesus has as broad a horizon as his Master. Jesus thought in continents and seas. His follower prays in continents and seas. This man does not know what is being accomplished. Yes! He *does* know, too. He knows by the inference of faith.

This room where we are meeting and talking together might be shut up so completely that no light comes in. A single crack breaking somewhere lets in a thin line of light. But that line of light shining in the darkness tells of a whole sun of light flooding the outer world.

There comes to this man occasional, yes frequent, evidences of changes being wrought, yet he knows that these are but the thin line of glory light which speaks of the fuller shining. And with a spirit touched with glad awe that he can and may help God, and a heart full alike of peace and of yearning, and a life fragrant with an unseen Presence he goes steadily on his way, towards the dawning of the day.

A Prehistoric Conflict.

In its simplest meaning prayer has to do with a conflict. Rightly understood it is the deciding factor in a spirt conflict. The scene of the conflict is the earth. The purpose of the conflict is to decide the control of the earth, and its inhabitants. The conflict runs back into the misty ages of the creation time.

The rightful prince of the earth is Jesus, the King's Son. There is a pretender prince who was once rightful prince. He was guilty of a breach of trust. But like King Saul, after his rejection and David's anointing in his place, he has been and is trying his best by dint of force to hold the realm and oust the rightful ruler.

The rightful Prince is seeking by utterly different means, namely by persuasion, to win the world back to its first allegiance. He had a fierce set-to with the pretender, and after a series of victories won the great victory of the resurrection morning.

There is one peculiarity of this conflict making it different from all others; namely, a decided victory, and the utter vanquishing of the leading general has not stopped the war. And the reason is remarkable. The Victor has a deep love-ambition to win, not merely against the enemy, but *into men's hearts, by their free consent.* And so, with marvellous love-born wisdom and courage, the conflict is left open, for men's sake.

It is a spirit conflict. The earth is swung in a spirit atmosphere. There are unnumbered thousands of spirit beings good and evil, tramping the earth's surface, and filling its atmosphere. They are splendidly organized into two compact organizations.

Man is a spirit being; an embodied spirit being. He has a body and a mind. He is a spirit. His real conflicts are of the spirit sort; in the spirit realm, with other spirit beings.

The only sort of power that influences in the spirit realm is *moral* power. By which is not meant *goodness,* but that sort of power either bad or good which is not of a physical sort: that higher, infinitely higher and greater power than the mere physical. Moral power is the opposite of violent or physical power.

God does not use force, violent physical force. There are some exceptions to this statement. There have been righteous wars, righteous on one side. Turning to the Bible record, in emergencies, in extreme instances God has ordered war measures. The nations that Israel was told to remove by the death of war would have inevitably worn themselves out through their physical excesses, and disobedience of the laws of life. But a wide view of the race revealed an emergency which demanded a speedier movement. And as an exception, for the sake of His plan for the ultimate saving of a race, and a world, God gave an extermination order. The emergency makes the exception. There is one circumstance under which the taking of human life is right, namely, when it can be clearly established that God the giver and sovereign of life has so directed. But the rule clearly is that God does not use force.

But note sharply in contrast with this that physical force is one of Satan's chief weapons. But mark there two intensely interesting facts: first, he can use it only as he secures man as his ally, and uses it through him. And, second, in using it he has with great subtlety sought to shift the sphere of action. He knows that in the sphere of spirit force pure and simple he is at a disadvantage: indeed, worse yet, he is defeated. For there is a moral force on the other side greater than any at his command. The forces of purity and righteousness he simply *can*not withstand. Jesus is the personification of purity and righteousness. It was on this moral ground, in this spirit sphere that He won the great victory. He ran a terrific gauntlet of tests, subtle and fierce, through those human years, and came out victor with His purity and righteousness unstained.

Prayer is Projecting One's Spirit Personality.

Now prayer is a spirit force. It has to do wholly with spirit beings and forces. It is an insistent claiming, by a man, an embodied spirit being, down on the contested earth, that the power of Jesus' victory over the great evil-spirit chieftain shall extend to particular lives now under his control. The prayer takes on the characteristic of the man praying. He is a spirit being. It becomes a spirit force. It is a projecting into the spirit realm of his spirit personality. Being a spirit force it has certain qualities or characteristics of unembodied spirit beings. An unembodied spirit being is not limited by space as we embodied folk are. It can go as swiftly as we can think. If I want to go to London it will take at least a week's time to get my body through the intervening space. But I can think myself into London more quickly than I can say the words, and be walking down the Strand. Now a spirit being can go as quickly as I can think.

Further, spirit beings are not limited by material obstructions such as the walls of this building. When I came in here to-day I came in by this door. You all came in by these doors. We were obliged to come in either by doors or windows. But the spirit beings who are here listening to us, and deeply concerned with our discussion did not bother with the doors. They came in through the walls, or the roof, if they were above us, or through the floor here, if they happened to be below this level.

Prayer has these qualities of spirit beings of not being limited by space, or by material obstacles. Prayer is really projecting my spirit, that is, my real personality to the spot concerned, and doing business there with other spirit beings. For example there is a man in a city on the Atlantic seaboard for whom I pray daily. It makes my praying for him very tangible and definite to recall that every time I pray my prayer is a spirit force instantly traversing the space in between him and me, and going without hindrance through the walls of the house where he is, and influencing the spirit beings surrounding him, and so influencing his own will.

When it became clear to me some few years ago that my Master would not have me go yet to those parts of the earth where the need is greatest, a deep tinge of disappointment came over me. Then as I realized the wisdom of His sovereignty in service, it came to me anew that I could exert a positive influence in those lands for Him by prayer. As many others have done, I marked out a daily schedule of prayer. There are certain ones for whom I pray by name, at certain intervals. And it gives great simplicity to my faith, and great gladness to my heart to remember that every time such prayer is breathed out, my spirit personality is being projected yonder, and in effect I am standing in Shanghai, and Calcutta and Tokyo in turn and pleading the power of Jesus' victory over the evil one there, and on behalf of those faithful ones standing there for God.

It is a fiercely contested conflict. Satan is a trained strategist, and an obstinate fighter. He refuses to acknowledge defeat until he must. It is the fight of his life. Strange as it must seem, and perhaps absurd, he apparently hopes to succeed. If we knew all, it might seem less strange and absurd, because of the factors on his side. There is surely much down in the world of the sort which we can fully appreciate to give colour to his expectations. Prayer is insisting upon Jesus' victory, and the retreat of the enemy on each particular spot, and heart and problem concerned.

The enemy yields only what he must. He yields only what is taken. Therefore the ground must be taken step by step. Prayer must be definite. He yields only when he must. Therefore the prayer must be persistent. He continually renews his attacks, therefore the ground taken must be *held* against him in the Victor's name. This helps to understand why prayer must be persisted in after we have full assurance of the result, and even after some immediate results have come, or, after the general results have commenced coming.

Giving God a Fresh Footing.

The Victor's best ally in this conflict is the man, who while he remains down on the battle-field, puts his life in full touch with his Saviour-Victor, and then incessantly, insistently, believingly claims *victory in Jesus' name.* He is the one foe among men whom Satan cannot withstand. He is projecting an irresistible spirit force into the spirit realm. Satan is obliged to yield. We are so accustomed through history's long record to seeing victories won through force, physical force, alone, that it is difficult for us to realize that moral force defeats as the other never can. Witness the demons in the gospels, and in modern days in China,[1] clearly against their own set purpose, Notwithstanding intensest struggle on their part obliged to admit defeat, and even to ask favours of their Conqueror. The records of personal Christian service give fascinating instances of fierce opposition utterly subdued and individuals transformed through such influence.

Had we eyes to see spirit beings and spirit conflicts we would constantly see the enemy's defeat in numberless instances through the persistent praying of some one allied to Jesus in the spirit of his life. Every time such a man prays it is a waving of the red-dyed flag of Jesus Christ above Satan's head in the spirit world. Every such man who freely gives himself over to God, and gives himself up to prayer is giving God a new spot in the contested territory on which to erect His banner of victory.

The Japanese struggled for weeks to get a footing on the Port Arthur peninsula, even after the naval victories had

---

[1] "Demon Possession," by J. L. Nevius.

practically rendered Russia helpless on the seas. It was an unusual spectacle to witness such difficulty in getting a landing after such victories. But with the bulldog tenacity that has marked her fighting Japan fought for a footing. Nothing could be done till a footing was gotten.

Prayer is man giving God a footing on the contested territory of this earth. The man in full touch of purpose with God praying, insistently praying—that man is God's footing on the enemy's soil. The man wholly given over to God gives Him a new sub-headquarters on the battlefield from which to work out. And the Holy Spirit within that man, on the new spot, will insist on the enemy's retreat in Jesus the Victor's name. That is prayer. Shall we not, every one of us, increase God's footing down upon His prodigal earth!

Prayer a War Measure.

This world is God's prodigal son. The heart of God's bleeds over His Prodigal. It has been gone so long, and the home circle is broken. He has spent all the wealth of His thought on a plan for winning the prodigal back home. Angels and men have marvelled over that plan, its sweep, its detail, its strength and wisdom, its tenderness. He needs man for His plan. He will *use* man. That is true. He will *honour* man in service. That is true. But these only touch the edge of the truth. The pathway from God to a human heart is through a human heart. When He came to the great strategic move in His plan, He Himself came down as a man and made that move. *He needs man for His plan.*

The greatest agency put into man's hands is prayer. To understand that at all fully one needs to define prayer. And to define prayer adequately one must use the language of war. Peace language is not equal to the situation. The earth is in a state of war. It is being hotly besieged and so one must use war talk to grasp the facts with which prayer is concerned. *Prayer from God's side is communication between Himself and His allies in the enemy's country.* Prayer is not persuading God. It does not influence God's purpose. It is not winning Him over to our side; never that. He is far more eager for what we are rightly eager for than we ever are. What there is of wrong and sin and suffering that pains you, pains Him far more. He knows more about it. He is more keenly sensitive to it than the most sensitive one of us. Whatever of heart yearning there may be that moves you to prayer is from Him. God takes the initiative in all prayer. It starts with Him. True prayer moves in a circle. It begins in the heart of God, sweeps down into a human heart upon the earth, so intersecting the circle of the earth, which is the battle-field of prayer, and then it goes back again to its starting point, having accomplished its purpose on the downward swing.

Three Forms of Prayer.

Prayer is the word commonly used for all intercourse with God. But it should be kept in mind that the word covers and includes three forms of intercourse. All prayer grows up through, and ever continues in three stages.

The first form of prayer is *communion*. That is simply being on good terms with God. It involves the blood of the cross as the basis of our getting and being on good terms. It involves my coming to God through Jesus. Communion is fellowship with God. Not request for some particular thing; not asking, but simply enjoying Himself, loving Him, thinking about Him, how beautiful, and intelligent, and strong and loving and lovable He is; talking to Him without words. That is the truest worship, thinking how worthy He is of all the best we can possibly bring to Him, and infinitely more. It has to do wholly with God and a man being on good terms with each other. Of necessity it includes confession on my part and forgiveness upon God's part, for only so can we come into the relation of fellowship. Adoration, worship belong to this first phase of prayer. Communion is the basis of all prayer. It is the essential breath of the true Christian life. It concerns just two, God and myself, yourself. Its influence is directly subjective. *It affects me.*

The second form of prayer is *petition*. And I am using that word now in the narrower meaning of asking something for one's self. Petition is definite request of God for something I need. A man's whole life is utterly dependent upon the giving hand of God. Everything we need comes from Him. Our friendships, ability to make money, health, strength in temptation, and in sorrow, guidance in difficult circumstances, and in all of life's movements; help of all sorts, financial, bodily, mental, spiritual—all come from God, and necessitate a constant touch with Him. There needs to be a constant stream of petition going up, many times wordless prayer. And there will be a constant return stream of answer and supply coming down. The door between God and one's own self must be kept ever open. The knob to be turned is on our side. He opened His side long ago, and propped it open, and threw the knob away. The whole life hinges upon this continual intercourse with our wondrous God. This is the second stage or form of prayer. It concerns just two: God and the man dealing with God. It is subjective in its influence: *its reach is within.*

The third form of prayer is *intercession.* True prayer never stops with petition for one's self. It reaches out for others. The very word intercession implies a reaching out for some one else. It is standing as a go-between, a mutual friend, between God and some one who is either out of touch with Him, or is needing special help. Intercession is the climax of prayer. It is the outward drive of prayer. It is the effective end of prayer *outward.* Communion and petition are upward and downward. Intercession rests upon these two as its foundation. Communion and petition store the life with the power of God; intercession lets it out on behalf of others. The first two are necessarily for self; this third is for others. They ally a man fully with God: it makes use of that alliance for others. Intercession is the full-bloomed plant whose roots and strength lie back and down in the other two forms. *It* is the form of prayer that helps God in His great love-plan for winning a planet back to its true sphere. It will help through these talks to keep this simple analysis of prayer in mind. For much that will be said will deal chiefly with this third form, intercession, the outward movement of prayer.

The Climax of Prayer.

To God man is first an objective point, and then, without ceasing to be that, he further becomes a distributing centre. God ever thinks of a man doubly: first for his own self, and then for his possible use in reaching others. Communion and petition fix and continue one's relation to God, and so prepare for the great outreaching form of prayer—intercession. Prayer must begin in the first two but reaches its climax in the third. Communion and petition are of necessity self-wide. Intercession is world-wide in its reach. And all true rounded prayer will ever have all three elements in it. There must be the touch with God. One's constant needs make constant petition. But the heart of the true follower has caught the warm contagion of the heart of God and reaches out hungrily for the world. Intercession is the climax of prayer.

Much is said of the subjective and objective value of prayer; its influence upon one's self, and its possible influence upon persons and events quite outside of one's self. Of necessity the first two sorts of prayer here named are subjective; they have to do wholly with one's self. Of equal necessity intercessory prayer is objective; it has to do wholly with others. There is even here a reflex influence; in the first two directly subjective; here incidentally reflex. Contact with God while dealing with him for another of necessity influences me. But that is the mere fringe of the garment. The main driving purpose is outward.

Just now in certain circles it seems quite the thing to lay great stress upon the subjective value of prayer and to whittle down small, or, deny entirely its value in influencing others. Some who have the popular ear are quite free with tongue and pen in this direction. From both without and within distinctly Christian circles their voices come. One wonders if these friends lay the greater emphasis on the subjective value of prayer so as to get a good deep breath for their hard drive at the other. Yet the greater probability is that they honestly believe as they say, but have failed to grasp the full perspective of the picture. In listening to such statements one remembers with vivid distinctness that the scriptural *standpoint* always is this: that things quite outside of one's self, that in the natural order of prevailing circumstances would not occur, are made to occur through prayer. Jesus constantly so *assumed*. The first-flush, commonsense view of successful prayer is that some actual result is secured through its agency.

it is an utter begging of the question to advance such a theory as a sufficient explanation of prayer. For prayer in its simplest conception supposes something changed that is not otherwise reachable. Both from the scriptural, and from a rugged philosophical standpoint the objective is the real driving point of all full prayer. The subjective is in order to the objective, as the final outward climactic reach of God's great love-plan for the world.

Six Facts Underlying Prayer.

It will help greatly to step back and up a bit for a fresh look at certain facts that underlie prayer. Everything depends on a right point of view. There may be many view-points, from which to study any subject; but of necessity any one view-point must take in all the essential facts concerned. If not, the impression formed will be wrong, and a man will be misled in his actions. In these talks I make no attempt to prove the Bible's statements, nor to suggest a common law for their interpretation. That would be a matter for quite a separate series of talks. It clears the ground to assume certain things. I am assuming the accuracy of these scriptural statements. And I am glad to say I have no difficulty in doing so.

Now there are certain facts constantly stated and assumed in this old Book. They are clearly stated in its history, they are woven into its songs, and they underlie all these prophetic writings, from Genesis clear to the end of John's Patmos visions. Possibly they have been so familiar and taken for granted so long as to have grown unfamiliar. The very old may need stating as though very new. Here is a chain of six facts:

First:—The earth is the Lord's and the fullness thereof.[1]

[1]Psalm 24:1.

His by creation and by sovereign rule. The Lord sat as King at the flood.[1]

Second:—God gave the dominion of the earth to man. The kingship of its life, the control and mastery of its forces.[2]

Third:—Man, who held the dominion of the earth in trust from God, transferred his dominion to somebody else, by an act which was a double act. He was deceived into doing that act. It was an act of disobedience and of obedience. Disobedience to God, and obedience to another one, a prince who was seeking to get the dominion of the earth into his own hands. That act of the first man did this. The disobedience broke with God, and transferred the allegiance from God. The obedience to the other one transferred the allegiance, and through that, the dominion to this other one.

The fourth fact is this:—The dominion or kingship of this earth so far as given to man, is now not God's, for He gave it to man. And it is not man's, for he has transferred it to another. It is in the control of that magnificent prince whose changed character supplies his name—Satan, the hater, the enemy. Jesus repeatedly speaks of "the prince"—that is the ruling one—"of this world."[3] John speaks in his vision-book of a time coming when "the kingdom (not kingdoms, as in the old version) of the world is become the kingdom of our Lord, and of His Christ."[4] By clear interference previous to that time it is somebody's else kingdom than His. The kingship or rulership of the earth which was given to man is now Satan's.

The fifth fact:—God was eager to swing the world back to its original sway: for His own sake for man's sake, for the earth's sake. You see, we do not know God's world as it came

---

[1] Psalm 29:10.

[2] Genesis 1: 26, 28. Psalms 8:6. See quotations of this, referring to the Man who will restore original conditions in 1 Cor. 15:27. Ephesians 1:22. Hebrews 2:8. Psalms 115:16.

[3] John 12:31; 14:30; 16:11.   [4] Revelation 11:15.

from His hand. It is a rarely beautiful world even yet—the stars above, the plant life, the waters, the exquisite colouring and blending, the combinations of all these—an exquisitely beautiful world even yet. But it is not the world it was, nor that some coming day it will be. It has been sadly scarred and changed under its present ruler. Probably Eve would not recognize in the present world her early home-earth as it came fresh from the hand of its maker.

God was eager to swing the old world back to its original control. But to do so He must get a man, one of the original trustee class through whom He might swing it back to its first allegiance. It was given to man. It was swung away by man. It must be swung back by man. And so a Man came, and while Jesus was perfectly and utterly human, we spell that word Man with a capital M because He was a man quite distinct from all men. Because He was more truly human than all other men He is quite apart from other men. This Man was to head a movement for swinging the world back to its first allegiance.

The sixth fact is this:—These two, God's Man, and the pretender-prince, had a combat: the most terrific combat ever waged or witnessed. From the cruel, malicious cradle attack until Calvary's morning and two days longer it ran. Through those thirty-three years it continued with a terrificness and intensity unknown before or since. The master-prince of subtlety and force did his best and his worst, through those Nazareth years, then into the wilderness,—and Gethsemane—and Calvary. And that day at three o'clock and for a bit longer the evil one thought he had won. And there was great glee up in the headquarters of the prince of this world. They thought the victory was theirs when God's Man lay in the grave under the bars of death, within the immediate control of the lord of death. But the third morning came and the bars of death were snapped like cotton thread. *Jesus rose a Victor.* For it was not possible that such as *He could be held by death's lord.* And then Satan knew that he was defeated. Jesus, God's Man, the King's rightful prince, had gotten the victory.

But, please mark very carefully four sub-facts on Satan's side. First, he refuses to acknowledge his defeat. Second, he refuses to surrender his dominion until he must. He yields only what he must and when he must. Third, he is supported in his ambitions by man. He has man's consent to his control. The majority of men on the earth to-day, and in every day, have assented to his control. He has control only through man's consent. (Satan *can*not get into a man's heart without his consent, and God *will* not.) And, fourth, he hopes yet to make his possession of the earth permanent.

The Victor's Great Plan.

Now, hold your breath and note, on the side of the Victor-prince, this unparalleled and unimitated action: He has left the conflict open, and the defeated chief on the field that He may win not simply against the chief, but through that victory may win the whole prodigal race back to His Father's home circle again. But the great pitched battle is yet to come. I would better say *a* pitched battle, for the greatest one is past. Jesus rides into the future fight a Victor. Satan will fight his last fight under the shadow and sting of a defeat. Satan is apparently trying hard to get a Jesus. That is to say Jesus was God's Man sent down to swing the world back. Satan is trying his best to get *a man*—one of the original trustee class, to whom the dominion of the earth was intrusted—a man who will stand for him even as Jesus stood for God. Indeed a man who will personify himself even as Jesus was the personification of God, the express image of His person. When he shall succeed in that the last desperate crisis will come.

Now prayer is this: A man, one of the original trustee class, who received the earth in trust from God, and who gave its control over to Satan; a man, *on the earth,* the poor old Satan-stolen, sin-slimed, sin-cursed, contested earth; a man, on the earth, *with his life in full touch with the Victor, and sheer out of touch with the pretender-prince, insistently claiming that Satan shall yeild before Jesus' victory, step by step, life after life.* Jesus is the victor. Satan knows it, and fears Him. He must yield before His advance, and he must yield before this man who stands for Jesus down on the earth. And he *will* yield. Reluctantly, angrily, as slowly as may be, stubbornly contesting every inch of ground, his clutches will loosen and he will go before this Jesus-man.

Jesus said "the prince of the world cometh: and he hath nothing in Me."[1] When you and I say, as we may say, very humbly depending on His grace, very determinedly in the resolution of our own imperial will, "though the prince of this world come he shall have nothing in me, no coaling station however small on the shores of my life," then we shall be in position where Satan must yeild as we claim—victory in the Victor's Name.

[1] John 14:30.

How God Gives.

Some one may object to all this that the statements of God's word do not agree with this point of view.

At random memory brings up a few very familiar passages, frequently quoted. "Call unto Me, and I will answer thee, and will shew thee great things, and difficult, that thou knowest not."[1] "And call upon Me in the day of trouble; I will deliver thee and thou shalt glorify Me."[2] "Ask, and it shall be given you; seek, and ye shall find; knock, and it shall be opened unto you."[3] Here it seems, as we have for generations been accustomed to think, that our asking is the thing that influences God to do. And further, that many times persistent, continued asking is necessary to induce God to do. And the usual explanation for this need of persistence is that God is testing our faith, and seeking to make certain changes in us, before granting our requests. This explanation is without doubt quite true, *in part.* Yet the thing to mark is that it explains *only* in part. And when the whole circle of truth is brought into view, this explanation is found to cover only a small part of the whole.

We seem to learn best about God by analogies. The analogy never brings all there is to be learned. Yet it seems to be the nearest we can get. From what we know of ourselves we come to know Him.

Will you notice how men give? Among those who give to benevolent enterprises there are three sorts of givers, with variations in each.

There is the man who gives because he is influenced by others. If the right man or committee of men call, and deftly present their pleas, playing skillfully upon what may appeal to him; his position; his egotism; the possible advantage to accrue; what men whom he wants to be classed with are doing, and so on through the wide range that such men are familiar with; if they persist, by and by he gives. At first he seems reluctant, but finally gives with more or less grace. That is one sort of giver.

There is a second sort: the man of truly benevolent heart who is desirous of giving that he may be of help to other men. He listens attentively when pleas come to him, and waits only long enough to satisfy himself of the worth of the cause, and the proper sort of amount to give, and then gives.

There is a third sort, the rarest sort. This second man a stage farther on, who *takes the initiative.* He looks about him, makes inquiries, and thinks over the great need in every direction of his fellow men. He decides where his money may best be used to help; and then himself offers to give. But his gift may be abused by some who would get his money if they could, and use it injudiciously, or otherwise than he intends. So he makes certain conditions which must be met, the purpose of which is to establish sympathetic relations in some particular with those whom he would help. An Englishman's heart is strongly moved to get the story of Jesus to the inland millions of Chinese. He requests the China-Inland Mission to control the expenditure of almost a million dollars of his money in such a way as best to secure the object in his heart. An American gives a large sum to the Young Men's Christian Association of his home city to be expended as directed. His thought is not to build up this particular organization, but to benefit large numbers of the young men of his town who will meet certain conditions which he thinks to be for their good. He has learned to trust this organization, and so it becomes his trustee.

Another man feels that if the people of New York City can be given good reading they can thereby best be helped in life. And so he volunteers money for a number of libraries throughout that city. And thousands who yearn to increase their knowledge come into sympathy with him in that one point through his gift. In all such cases the giver's thought is to accomplish certain results in those whose purpose in certain directions is sympathetic with his own.

Any human illustration of God must seem crude. Yet of these three sorts of givers there is one and only one that begins to suggest how God gives. It may seem like a very sweeping statement to make, yet I am more and more disposed to believe it true that *most persons* have unthinkingly thought of God's answering prayer as the first of these three men give. Many others have had in mind some such thought as the second suggests. Yet to state the case even thus definitely is to make it plain that neither of these ways in any manner illustrate God's giving. The third comes the nearest to picturing the God who hears and answers prayer. Our God has a great heart yearning after His poor prodigal world, and after each one in it. He longs to have the effects of sin removed, and the original image restored. He takes the initiative. Yet everything that is done for man must of necessity be through man's will; by his free and glad consent. The obstacles in the way are not numberless nor insurmountable, but they are many and they are stubborn. There is a keen, cunning pretender-prince who is a past-master in the fine art of handling men. There are wills warped and weakened; consciences blurred; minds the opposite of keen, sensibilities whose edge has been dulled beyond ordinary hope of being ever made keen again. Sin has not only stained the life, but warped the judgment, sapped the will, and blurred the mental vision. And God has a hard time just because every change must of necessity be through that sapped and warped will.

Yet the difficulty though great is never complex but very simple. And so the statement of His purpose is ever exquisitely simple. Listen again: "Call unto Me, and I will answer thee and shew thee great things and difficult which thou knowest not." If a man *call* he has already turned his face towards God. His will has acted, and acted doubly; away from the opposite, and *towards* God, a simple step but a tremendous one. The calling is the point of sympathetic contact with God where their purposes become the same. The caller is beset by difficulties and longs for freedom. The God who speaks to him saw the difficulties long ago and eagerly longed to remove them. Now they have come to agreement. And through this willing will God eagerly works out His purpose.

A Very Old Question.

This leads to a very old question: Does prayer influence God? No question has been discussed more, or more earnestly. Skeptical men of fine scientific training have with great positiveness said "no." And Christian men of scholarly training and strong faith have with equal positiveness said "yes." Strange to say both have been right. Not right in all their statements, nor right in all their beliefs, nor right in all their processes of thinking, but right in their ultimate conclusions as represented by these short words, "no," and "yes." Prayer does not influence God. Prayer surely does influence God. It does not influence His purpose. It does influence His action. Everything that ever has been prayed for, of course I mean every right thing, God has already purposed to do. But He does nothing without our consent. He has been hindered in His purposes by our lack of willingness. When we learn His purposes and make them our prayers we are giving Him the opportunity to act. It is a double opportunity: manward and Satanward. We are willing. Our willingness checkmates Satan's opposition. It opens the path to God and rids it of the obstacles. And so the road is cleared for the free action already planned.

The further question of nature's laws being sometimes set aside is wholly a secondary matter. Nature's laws are merely God's habit of action in handling secondary forces. They involve no purpose of God. His purposes are regarding moral issues. That the sun shall stay a bit longer than usual over a certain part of the earth is a mere detail with God. It does not affect His power for the whole affair is under His finger. It does not affect His purpose for that is concerning far more serious matters. The emergencies of earth wrought by sin necessitate just such incidents, that the great purpose of God for man shall be accomplished.

Emergencies change all habits of action, divine and human. They are the real test of power. If a man throw down the bundle he is carrying and make a quick wild dash out into the middle of the street, dropping his hat on the way, and grasp convulsively for something on the ground when no cause appears for such action we would quickly conclude that the proper place for him is an asylum. But if a little toddling child is almost under the horse's hoofs, or the trolley car, no one thinks of criticising, but instead admires his courage, and quick action, and breathlessly watches for the result. Emergencies call for special action. They should control actions, where they exist. Emergencies explain action, and explain satisfactorily what nothing else could explain.

The world is in a great emergency through sin. Only as that tremendous fact grips us shall we be men of prayer, and men of action up to the limit of the need, and to the limit of the possibilities. Only as that intense fact is kept in mind shall we begin to understand God's actions in history, and in our personal experiences. The greatest event of earth, the cross, was an emergency action.

The fact that prayer does not make any change in God's thought or purpose, reveals His marvellous love in a very tender way.

Suppose I want something very much and *need* as well as want. And I go to God and ask for it. And suppose He is reluctant about giving: had not thought about giving me that thing; and rather hesitates. But I am insistent, and plead and persist and by and by God is impressed with my earnestness, and sees that I really need the thing, and answers my prayer, and gives me what I ask. Is not that a loving God so to listen and yield to my plea? Surely. How many times just such an instance has taken place between a child and his father, or mother. And the child thinks to himself, "How loving father is; he has given me the thing I asked for."

But suppose God is thinking about me all the time, and planning, with love-plans for me, and longing to give me much that He has. Yet in His wisdom He does not give because *I* do not know my own need, and have not opened my hand to receive, yes, and, further yet, likely as not, not knowing my need I might abuse, or misuse, or fail to use, something given before I had felt the need of it. And now I come to see and feel that need and come and ask and He, delighted with the change in me, eagerly gives. Tell me, is not that a very much more loving God than the other conception suggests? The truth is *that* is God. Jesus says, "Your Father knoweth what things ye have need of *before ye ask.*" And He is a Father. And with God the word father means mother too. Then what He *knows* we need He has *already planned* to give. The great question for me then in praying for some personal thing is this: Do *I* know what *He* knows I need? Am I thinking about what He is thinking about for me?

And then remembering that God is so much more in His loving planning than the wisest, most loving father we know. Does a mother think into her child's needs, the food, and clothing and the extras too, the luxuries? That is God, only He is more loving and wiser than the best of us. I have sometimes thought this: that if God were to say to me: "I want to give you something as a special love-gift; an extra because I love you: what would you like to have?" Do you know I have thought I would say, "Dear God, *you* choose. *I* choose what *you* choose." He is thinking about me. He knows what I am thinking of, and what I would most enjoy, and He is such a lover-God that He would choose something just a bit finer than I would think. I might be thinking of a dollar, but likely as not He is thinking of a double eagle. I am thinking of blackberries, big, juicy blackberries, but really I do not know what blackberries are beside the sort He knows and would choose for me. That is our God. Prayer does not and cannot change the purpose of such a God. For every right and good thing we might ask for He has already planned to give us. But prayer does change the action of God. Because He cannot give against our wills, and our willingness as expressed by our asking gives Him the opportunity to do as He has already planned.

The Greatest Prayer.

There is a greatest prayer, *the* greatest that can be offered. It is the substratum of every true prayer. It is the undercurrent in the stream of all Spirit-breathed prayer. Jesus Himself gives it to us in the only form of prayer He left for our use. It is small in size, but mighty in power. Four words—"Thy will be done." Let us draw up our chairs, and *brew* it over mentally, that its strength and fragrance may come up into our nostrils, and fill our very beings.

"Thy": That is God. On one side, He is wise, with all of the intellectual strength, and keenness and poised judgment that word among men brings to us. On another side, He is strong, with all that that word can imply of might and power irresistible. On still another side He is good, pure, holy with the finest thought those words ever suggest to us in those whom we know best, or in our dreams and visions. Then on a side remaining, the tender personal side, He is—loving? No, that is quite inadequate. He is *love*. Its personification is He. Now remember that we do not know the meaning of those words. Our best definition and thought of them, even in our dreams, when we let ourselves out, but hang around the outskirts. The heart of them we do not know. Those words mean infinitely more than we think. Their meaning is a projection along the lines of our thought of them, but measurelessly

beyond our highest reach.

And then, this God, wise, strong, good, and love, *is kin to us.* We belong to Him.

> "We are His flock;
> He doth us feed.
> And for His sheep,
> He doth us take."

We are His children by creation, and by a new creation in Jesus Christ. He is ours, by His own act. That is the "Thy"—a God wise, strong, pure, who is love, and who is a Father-mother-God, and is *our* God.

"Thy *will.*" God's will is His desires, His purposes, that which He wishes to occur, and that to which He gives His strength that it may occur. The earth is His creation. Men are His children. Judging from wise loving parents among men He has given Himself to thinking and studying and planning for all men, and every man, and for the earth. His plan is the most wise, pure, loving plan that can be thought of, *and more.* It takes in the whole sweep of our lives, and every detail of them. Nothing escapes the love-vigilance of our God. What *can* be so vigilant and keen as love? Hate, the exact reverse, comes the nearest. It is ever the extremes that meet. But hate cannot come up to love for keen watchfulness at every turn. Health, strength, home, loved ones, friendships, money, guidance, protecting care, the necessities, the extras that love ever thinks of, service—all these are included in God's loving thought for us. That is His will. It is modified by the degree of our conset, and further modified by the circumstances of our lives. Life has become a badly tangled skein of threads. God with infinite patience and skill is at work untangling and bringing the best possible out of the tangle. What is absolutely best is rarely relatively best. That which is best in itself is usually not best under certain circumstance. He could oftentimes do more, and do it in much less time if our human wills were more pliant to His. He can be trusted. And of course *trust* means *trust in the darkest dark* where you cannot see. And trust means trust. It does not mean test. Where you trust you do not test. Where you test you do not trust. Making this our prayer means trusting God. That is God, and that His will, and that the meaning of our offering this prayer.

"Thy will *be.*" A man's will is the man in action, within the limits of his power. God's will for man is Himself in action, within the limits of our cooperation. *Be* is a verb, an action-word, in the passive voice. It takes some form of the verb to be to express the passive voice of any action-word. It takes the intensest activity of will to put this passive voice into human action. The greatest strength is revealed in intelligent yielding. Here the prayer is expressing the utter willingness of a man that God's will shall be done in him, and through him. A man never *loses* his will, unless indeed he lose his manhood. But here he makes that will as strong as it can be made, as a bit of steel, better like the strong oak, strong enough to sway and bend in the wind. Then he uses all its strength in becoming passive to a higher will. And that too when the purpose of that higher will is not clear to his own limited knowledge and understanding.

"Thy will be *done.*" That is, be accomplished, be brought to pass. The word stands for the action in its perfected, finished state. Thy will be fully accomplished in its whole sweep and in all its items. It speaks not only the earnest desire of the heart praying, but the set purpose that everything in the life is held subject to the doing of this purpose of God. It means that surrender of purpose that has utterly changed the lives of the strongest men in order that the purpose of God might be dominant. It cut off from a great throne earth's greatest jurist, the Hebrew lawgiver, and led him instead to be allied to a race of slaves. It led that intellectual giant

Jeremiah from an easy enjoyable leadership to espouse a despised cause and so be himself despised. It led Paul from the leadership of his generation in a great nation to untold suffering, and to a block and an ax. It led Jesus the very Son of God, away from a kingship to a cross. In every generation it has radically changed lives, and life-ambitions. "Thy will be done" is the great dominant purpose-prayer that has been the pathway of God in all His great doings among men.

That will is being done everywhere else in God's great world of worlds, save on the earth and that portion of the spirit world allied to this earth. Everywhere else there is the perfect music of harmony with God's will. Here only is heard the harsh discordant note.

With this prayer go two clauses that really particularize and explain it. They are included in it, and are added to make more clear the full intent. The first of these clauses gives the sweep of His will in its broadest outlines. The second touches the opposition to that will both for our individual lives and for the race and the earth.

The first clause is this, "Thy kingdom come." In both of these short sentences, "Thy will be done," "Thy kingdom come," the emphatic word is "Thy." That word is set in sharpest possible contrast here. There is another kingdom now on the earth. There is another will being done. This other kingdom must go if God's kingdom is to come. These kingdoms are antagonistic at every point of contact. They are rivals for the same allegiance and the same territory. They cannot exist together. Charles II and Cromwell cannot remain in London together. "Thy kingdom come," of necessity includes this, "the other kingdom go." "Thy kingdom come" means likewise "Thy king come," for in the nature of things there cannot be a kingdom without a king. That means again by the same inference, "the other prince go," the one who makes pretensions to being rightful heir to the throne. "Thy will be done" includes by the same inference this:—

"the other will be undone." This is the first great explanatory clause to be connected with this greatest prayer, "Thy kingdom come." It gives the sweep of God's will in its broadest outlines.

The second clause included in the prayer, and added to make clear the swing of action is this—"deliver us from the evil one." These two sentences, "Thy will be done," and "deliver us from the evil one," are naturally connected. Each statement includes the other. To have God's will fully done in us means emancipation from every influence of the evil one, either direct or indirect, or by hereditary taint. To be delivered from the evil one means that every thought and plan of God for our lives shall be fully carried out.

There are the two great wills at work in the world ever clashing in the action of history and in our individual lives. In many of us, aye, in all of us, though in greatly varying degree, these two wills constantly clash. Man is the real battle-field. The pitch of the battle is in his will. God will not do His will in a man without the man's will consenting. And Satan cannot. At the root the one thing that works against God's will is the evil one's will. And on the other hand the one thing that effectively thwarts Satan's plans is a man wholly given up to God's will.

The greatest prayer then fully expressed, sweeps first the whole field of action, then touches the heart of the action, and then attacks the opposition. It is this:—Thy kingdom come: Thy will be done: deliver us from the evil one. Every true prayer ever offered comes under this simple comprehensive prayer. It may be offered, it *is* offered with an infinite variety of detail. It is greatest because of its sweep. It includes all other petitions, for God's will includes everything for which prayer is rightly offered. It is greatest in its intensity. It hits the very bull's-eye of opposition to God.

II. HINDRANCES TO PRAYER

Why the Results Fail

Breaking with God.

God answers prayer. Prayer is God and man joining hands to secure some high end. He joins with us through the communication of prayer in accomplishing certain great results. This is the main drive of prayer. Our asking and expecting and God's doing jointly bring to pass things that otherwise would not come to pass. Prayer changes things. This is the great fact of prayer.

Yet a great many prayers are not answered. Or, to put it more accurately, a great many prayers fail utterly of accomplishing any results. Probably it is accurate to say that *thousands* of prayers go up and bring nothing down. This is certainly true. Let us say it just as bluntly and plainly as it can be said. As a result many persons are saying: "Well, prayer is not what you claim for it: we prayed and no answer came: nothing was changed."

From all sorts of circles, and in all sorts of language comes this statement. Scholarly men who write with wisdom's words, and thoughtless people whose thinking never even pricks the skin of the subject, and all sorts of people in between group themselves together here. And they are right, quite right. The bother is that what they say is not all there is to be said. There is yet more to be said, that is right too, and that changes the final conclusion radically. Partial truth is a very mean sort of lie.

The prayer plan like many another has been much disturbed, and often broken. And one who would be a partner with God up to the limit of his power must understand the things that hinder the prayer plan. There are three sorts of hindrances to prayer. First of all there are things in us that *break off connection* with God, the source of the changing power. Then there are certain things in us that *delay, or diminish* the results; that interfere with the full swing of the prayer plan of operations. And then there is a great *outside* hindrance to be reckoned upon. To-day we want to talk together of the first of these,

namely, the hindrances that *break off connections* between
God and His human partner.

Here again there is a division into three. There are three
things directly spoken of in the book of God that hinder
prayer. One of these is a familiar thing. What a pity that
repugnant things may become so familiar as no longer to
repel. It is this:—*sin* hinders prayer. In Isaiah's first chapter
God Himself speaking says, "When you stretch out your
hands"—the way they prayed, standing with outstretched
hands—"I will shut My eyes; when you make many prayers, I
will shut My ears."[1] Why? What's the difficulty? These
outstretched hands are *soiled!* They are actually holding their
sin-soiled hands up into God's face; and He is compelled to
look at the thing most hateful to Him. In the fifty-ninth
chapter of this same book,[2] God Himself is talking again.
Listen "Behold! the *Lord's* hand is not shortened: *His* ear is
not heavy." There is no trouble on the *up* side. God is all
right. "But"—listen with both your ears—"Your *iniquities*
...your *sins*...your *hands*...your *fingers*...your *lips*...
your *tongue*..." the slime of sin is oozing over everything!
Turn back to that sixty-sixth Psalm[3]—"if I regard iniquity in
my heart the Lord will not hear me." How much more if the
sin of the heart get into the hands or the life! And the fact to
put down plainly in blackest ink once for all this—*sin hinders
prayer.* There is nothing surprising about this. That we can
think the reverse is the surprising thing. Prayer is transacting
business with God. Sin is *breaking with God.*

Suppose I had a private wire from my apartments here to
my home in Cleveland, and some one should go outside and
drag the wire down until it touches the ground—a good
square touch with the ground—the electricians would call it
grounded, could I telegraph over that wire? Almost any child
knows I could not. Suppose some one *cuts* the wire, a good

[1]Isaiah 1:15.   [2]Isaiah 59:1-3.   [3]Psalm 66:18.

clean cut; the two ends are apart: not a mile; not a yard; but distinctly apart. Could I telegraph on that wire? Of course not. yet I might sit in my room and tick away by the hour wholly absorbed, and use most beautiful persuasive language—what is the good? The wire's cut. All my fine pleading goes into the ground, or the air. Now *sin cuts the wire;* it runs the message into the ground.

"Well," some one will object, "now you're cutting us all out, are you not? Are we not all conscious of a sinful something inside here that has to be fought, and held under all the while?" It certainly seems to be true that the nearer a man gets to God the more keenly conscious he is of a sinful tendency within even while having continual victory. But plainly enough what the Book means here is this:—if I am holding something in my life that the Master does not like, if I am failing to obey when His voice has spoken, that to me is sin. It may be wrong in itself. It may *not* be wrong in itself. It may not be wrong for another. Sometimes it is not the thing involved but the One involved that makes the issue. If that faithful quiet inner voice has spoken and I know what the Master would prefer and I fail to keep in line, that to me is sin. Then prayer is useless; sheet waste of breath. Aye, worse, it is deceptive. For I am apt to say or think, "Well, I am not as good as you, or you, but then I am not so bad; *I pray.*" And the truth is because I have broken with God the praying—saying words in that form—is utterly worthless.

You see *sin is slapping God in the face.* It may be polished, cultured sin. Sin seems capable of taking quite a high polish. Or it may be the common gutter stuff. A man is not concerned about the grain of a club that strikes him a blow. How can He and I talk together if I have done that, and stick to it—not even apologized. And of what good is an apology if the offense is being repeated. And if we cannot talk together of course working together is out of the question. And prayer is working together with God. Prayer is *pulling with God* in His plan for a world.

Shall we not put out the thing that is wrong? or put in the thing the Master wants in? For *Jesus'* sake? Aye for *Men's* sake: poor befooled men's sake who are being kept out and away because God cannot get at them through us!

Shall we bow and ask forgiveness for our sin, and petty stubbornness that has been thwarting the Master's love-plan? And yet even while we ask forgiveness there are lives out yonder warped and dwarfed and worse because of the hindrance in us; yes, and remaining so as we slip out of this meeting. May the fact send us out to walk very softly these coming days.

A Coaling Station for Satan's Fleet.

There is a second thing that is plainly spoken of that hinders prayer. James speaks of it in his letter.[1] "Ye have not because ye *ask* not"—that explains many parched up lives and churches and unsolved problems: no pipe lines run up to tap the reservoir, and give God an opening into the troubled territory. Then he pushes on to say—Ye ask, *and receive not*"—ah! there's just the rub; it is evidently an old story, this thing of not receiving—why? "because ye ask amiss to spend it *in your pleasures.*" That is to say selfish praying; asking for something just because I want it; want it for myself.

Here is a mother praying for her boy. He is just growing up towards young manhood; not a Christian boy yet; but a good boy. She is thinking, "I want *my* boy to be an honour to me; he bears my name; my blood is in his veins; I don't want my boy to be a prodigal. I want him to be a fine man, an honour to the family; and if he is a true Christian, he likely will be; *I wish he were a Christian.*" And so she prays, and prays repeatedly and fervently. God might touch her boy's heart and say, "I want you out here in India to help win my pro-

---

[1] James 4:2,3.

digal world back." *Oh!* she did not mean that! *Her* boy in far, far off *India!* Oh, no! Not that!! Yes, what *she* wanted—that was the whole thought—selfishness; the stream turning in to a dead sea within her own narrow circle; no thought of sympathy with God in His eager outreach for His poor sin-befooled world. The prayer itself in its object is perfectly proper, and rightly offered and answered times without number; but the *motive* wholly, uglily selfish and the selfishness itself becomes a foothold for Satan and so the purpose of the prayer is thwarted.

Here is a wife praying that her husband might become a Christian. Perhaps her thought is: "I wish John *were* a Christian: it would be so good: it really seems the proper thing: he would go to church with me, and sit in the pew Sunday morning: I'd like that." Perhaps she thinks: "He would be careful about swearing; he would quit drinking; and be nicer and gentler at home." Maybe she thinks: "He would ask a blessing at the meals; that would be so nice." Maybe she thinks: "We would have family prayers." *Maybe* that does not occur to her these days. This is what I say: *If* her thought does not go beyond some such range, of course *you* would say it is selfish. She is thinking of herself; not of the loving grieved God against whom her husband is in rebellion; not of the real significance to the man. God might touch her husband's heart, and then say: "I want you to help Me win My poor world back." And the change would mean a reduced income, and a different social position. *Oh!* she had not meant *that!* Yes—what *she* wanted for herself!

Here is a minister praying for a revival in his church. Maybe he is thinking; no, not exactly thinking; it is just half thinking itself out in his sub-consciousness—"I wish we had a good revival in our church; increased membership; larger attendance; easier finances; maybe an extra hundred or two in my own pocket; increased prestige in the denomination; a better call or appointment: I wish we might have a revival."

Now no true minister ever talked that way even to himself or deliberately thought it. To do so would be to see the mean contemptibility of it. But you know how sly we all are in our underneath scarcely-thought-out thoughts. This is what I say: *if* that be the sort of thing underneath a man's praying of course the motive is utterly selfish; a bit of the same thing that brought Satan his change of name and character.

Please notice that the reason for the prayer not being answered here is not an arbitrary reluctance upon God's part to do a desirable thing. He never fails to work whenever He has a half chance as far as it is possible to work, even through men of faulty conceptions and mixed motives. The reason lies much deeper. It is this: selfishness gives Satan a footing. It gives a coaling station for his fleet on the shore of your life. And of course he does his best to prevent the prayer, or when he cannot wholly prevent, to spoil the results as far as he can.

Prayer may properly be offered—*will* be properly offered for many wholly personal things; for physical strength, healing in sickness, about dearly loved ones, money needed; indeed regarding things that may not be necessary but only desirable and enjoyable, for ours is a loving God who would have His dear ones enjoy to the full their lives down here. But the *motive* determines the propriety of such requests. Where the whole purpose of one's life is *for Him* these things may be asked for freely as His gracious Spirit within guides. And there need be no bondage of morbid introspection, no continual internal rakings. *He knows if the purpose of the heart is to please Him.*

The Shortest Way to God.

A third thing spoken of as hindering prayer is an unforgiving spirit. You have noticed that Jesus speaks much about prayer and also speaks much about forgiveness. But have you noticed how, over and over again He *couples* these two— prayer *and* forgiveness? I used to wonder Why. I do not so much now. Nearly everywhere evidence keeps slipping in of the sore spots. One may try to keep his lips closed on certain subjects, but it seems about impossible to keep the ears entirely shut. And continually the evidence keeps sifting in revealing the thin skin, raw flesh, wounds never healed over, and some jaggedly open, almost everywhere one goes. Jesus' continual references reveal how strikingly alike is the oriental and the occidental; the first and the twentieth centuries.

Run through Matthew alone a moment. Here in the fifth chapter:[1] "If thou are coming to the altar"—that is approaching God; what we call prayer—"and rememberest that thy brother hath aught *against thee*"—that side of it—"leave there thy gift and go thy way, *first* be reconciled," and so on. Here comes a man with a lamb to offer. He approaches solemnly, reverently, towards the altar of God. But as he is coming there flashes across his mind the face of *that man,* with whom he has had difficulty. And instantly he can feel his grip tightening on the offering, and his teeth shutting closer at the quick memory. Jesus says, "If that be so lay your lamb right down." What! go abruptly away! Why! how the folks around the temple will talk! "Lay the lamb right down, and go thy way." The shortest way to God for that man is not the way to the altar, but around by that man's house. "*First,* be reconciled"—keep your perspective straight—follow the right order—"*first* be reconciled"—not *second; "then* come and offer thy gift."

In the sixth chapter[2] He gives the form of prayer which we commonly call the Lord's prayer. It contains seven petitions. At the close He stops to emphasize just one of the seven. You remember which one; the only about forgiveness. In the eighteenth chapter[3] Jesus is talking alone with the disciples about prayer; and he asks a question. It is never difficult to think of Peter asking a question or making a few remarks. He says,

[1]Matthew 5:23, 24.   [2]Matthew 6:9-15.   [3]Matthew 18:19-35.

"Master, how many times *must* I forgive a man? *Seven* times!" Apparently Peter thinks he is growing in grace. He can actually *think* now of forgiving a man seven times in succession. But the Master in effect says, "Peter, you haven't caught the idea. Forgiveness is not a question of mathematics; not a matter of *keeping tab* on somebody: not seven times but *seventy times seven.*" And Peter's eyes bulge open with an incredulous stare—"four hundred and ninety times!...one man—straightway!!" Apparently the Master is thinking, that he will lose count, or get tired of counting and conclude that forgiveness is preferable, or else by practice *breathe in the spirit of forgiveness—the* thing He meant.

Then as He was so fond of doing Jesus told a story to illustrate His meaning. A man owed his lord a great debt, twelve millions of dollars; that is to say practically an *unpayable* amount. By comparison with money to-day, in the western world, it would be about twelve billions. And he went to him and asked for time. He said: "I'm short just now; but I mean to pay; I don't mean to shirk: be easy with me; and I'll pay up the whole sum in time." And his lord generously forgave him the whole debt. That is Jesus' picture of God, as He knows Him who knows Him best. Then this forgiven man went out and found a fellow servant who owed him—how much do you think? Have you ever thought that Jesus had a keen sense of ludicrous? Surely it shows here. He owed him about sixteen dollars and a-quarter or a-half! And you can almost feel the clutch of this fellow's fingers on the other's throat as he sternly demands:—"Pay me that thou owest." And his fellow earnestly replies, "Please be easy with me; I mean to pay; I'm rather short just now: but I'm not trying to shirk; be easy with me." Is it possible the words do not sound familiar! But he would not, but put him in the jail. The last place to pay a debt! That is Jesus' picture of man as He knows him who knows him best. And in effect He says what we have been forgiven by God is as an unpayable amount.

And what are not willing to forgive is like sixteen dollars and a fraction by contrast. What little puny folks some of us are in our thinking and feeling!

"Oh, well," some one says, "you do not know how hard it is to forgive." You think not? I know this much:—that some persons, and some things you *cannot* forgive of yourself. But I am glad to say that I know this too that if one allows the Spirit of Jesus to sway the heart He will make you love persons you *can*not like. No natural affinity or drawing together through disposition, but a real yearning love in the heart. Jesus' love, when allowed to come in as freely as He means, fills your heart with pity for the man who has wounded you. An infinite, tender pity that he has sunk so low as to be capable of such actions.

But the fact to put down in the sharpest contrast of white and black is that we must forgive freely, frankly, generously, *"even as God,"* if we are to be in prayer touch with God.

And the reason is not far to find; a double reason, God-ward and Satanward. If prayer be partnership in the highest sense then the same spirit must animate both partners, the human and the divine, if the largest results are to come. And since unforgiveness roots itself down in hate Satan has room for both feet in such a heart with all the leeway in action of such purchase. That word *unforgiving!* What a group of relatives it has, near and far! Jealousy, envy, bitterness, the cutting word, the polished shaft of sarcasm with the poisoned tip, the green eye, the acid saliva—what kinsfolk these!

Search Me.

Sin, selfishness, an unforgiving spirit—what searchlights these words are! Many a splendid life to-day is an utter cipher in the spirit atmosphere because of some such hindrance. And God's great love-plan for His prodigal world is being held back; and lives being lost even where ultimately souls shall be saved because of the lack of human prayer partners.

May we not well pray:—Search me, oh God, and know my heart and help me know it; try me and know my innermost, undermost thoughts and purposes and ambitions, and help me know them; and see what way there be in me that is grief to Thee; and then lead me—and here the prayer may be a purpose as well as a prayer—lead me out of that way unto *Thy* way, *the* way everlasting. For Jesus' sake; aye for men's sake. too.

God's Pathway to Human Hearts.

God touches men through men. The Spirit's path to a human heart is through another human heart. With reverence be it said, yet with blunt plainness that in His plan for winning men to their true allegiance God is limited by the human limitations. That may seem to mean more than it really does. For our thought of the human is of the scarred, warped, shrivelled humanity that we know, and great changes come when God's Spirit controls. But the fact is there, however limited our understanding of it.

God needs man for His plan. That is the fact that stands out strong in thinking about prayer. God's greatest agency; man's greatest agency, for defeating the enemy and winning men back is intercession. God is counting mightily upon that. And He can count most mightily upon the man that faithfully practices that.

The results He longs for are being held back, and made smaller because so many of us have not learned how to pray simply and skilfully. We need training. And God understands that. He Himself will train. But we must be willing; actively willing. And just there the great bother comes in. A strong will perfectly yielded to God's will, or perfectly willing to be yielded, is His mightiest ally in redeeming the world.

Answers to prayer are delayed, or denied, out of kindness, *or,* that more may be given, *or,* that a far larger purpose may be served. But deeper down by far than that is this: *God's purposes are being delayed;* delayed because of our unwillingness to learn how to pray, *or,* our slowness—I almost said —our stupidity in learning. It is a small matter that my prayer be answered, or unanswered; not small to me; everything perhaps to me; but small in proportion. It is a tremendous thing that *God's purpose* for a world is being held back through my lack. The thought that prayer is *getting things* from God; chiefly that, is so small, pitiably small, and yet so common. The true conception understands that prayer is partnership with God in His planet-sized purposes, and includes the "all things" beside, as an important detail of the whole.

The real reason for the delay or failure lies simply in the difference between God's viewpoint and ours. In our asking either we have not reached the *wisdom* that asks best, *or,* we have not reached the *unselfishness* that is willing to sacrifice a good thing, for a better, or the best; the unselfishness that is willing to sacrifice the smaller personal desire for the larger thing that affects the lives of many.

We learn best by pictures, and by stories which are pen or word pictures. This was Jesus' favourite method of teaching. There are in the Bible four great, striking instances of delayed, or qualified answers to prayer. There are some others; but these stand out sharply, and perhaps include the main teachings of all. Probably all the instances of hindered prayer with which we are familiar will come under one of these. That is to say, where there are good connections upward as suggested in our last talk, *and,* excepting those that come under the talk succeeding this, namely, the great outside hindrance. These four are Moses' request to enter Canaan; Hannah's prayer for a son; Paul's thorn; and Jesus' prayer in Gethsemane.

Let us look a bit at these in turn.

For the Sake of a Nation

First is the incident of Moses' ungranted petition. Moses was the leader of his people. He is one of the giants of the human race from whatever standpoint considered. His codes are the basis of all English and American jurisprudence. From his own account of his career, the secret of all his power as a maker of laws, the organizer of a strangely marvellous nation, a military general and strategist—the secret of all was in his direct communication with God. He was peculiarly a man of prayer. Everything was referred to God, and he declared that everything—laws, organization, worship, plans—came to him from God. In national emergencies where moral catastrophe was threatened he petitioned God and the plans were changed in accordance with his request. He makes personal requests and they are granted. He was peculiarly a man who dealt directly with God about every sort of thing, national and personal, simple and complex. The record commonly credited to him puts prayer as the simple profound explanation of his stupendous career and achievements. He prayed. God worked along the line of his prayer. The great things recorded are the result. That is the simple inferential summary.

Now there is one exception to all this in Moses' life. It stands out the more strikingly that it is an exception; the one exception of a very long line. Moses asked repeatedly for one thing. It was not given him. God is not capricious nor arbitrary. There must be a reason. *There is*. And it is fairly luminous with light.

Here are the facts. These freed men of Egypt are a hard lot to lead and to live with. Slow, sensuous, petty, ignorant, narrow, impulsive, strangers to self-control, critical, exasperating—what an undertaking God had to make a nation, *the* nation of history, about which centred His deep reaching, far-seeing love ambition for redeeming a world out of such stuff! Only paralleled by the church being built upon such men as these Galilean peasants! What victories these! What a God to do such things! Only a God could do either and both! What immense patience it required to shape this people. What patience God has. Moses had learned much of patience in the desert sands with his sheep; for he had learned much of God. But the finishing touches were supplied by the grindstone of friction with the fickle temper of this mob of exslaves.

Here are the immediate circumstances. They lacked water.

They grew very thirsty. It was a serious matter in those desert sands with human lives, and young children, and the stock. No, it was not serious: really a very small matter, for *God was along,* and the enterprise was of His starting. It was His affair, all this strange journey. And they knew Him quite well enough in their brief experience to be expecting something fully equal to all needs with a margin thrown in. There was that series of stupendous things before leaving Egypt. There was the Red Sea, and fresh food daily delivered at every man's tent door, and game, juicy birds, brought down within arms' reach, yes, and—surely this alone were enough—there was living, cool water gushing abundantly, gladly out of the very heart of a flinty rock—if such a thing can be said to have a heart! Oh, yes it was a very small matter to be lacking anything with such a lavish God along.

But they forgot. Their noses were keener than their memories. They had better stomachs than hearts. The odorous onions of Egypt made more lasting impressions than this tender, patient, planning God. Yet here even their stomachs forgot those rock-freed waters. These people must be kinsfolk of ours. They seem to have some of the same family traits.

Listen: they begin to complain, to criticise. God patiently says nothing but provides for their needs. But Moses has not yet reached the high level that later experiences brought him. He is standing to them for God. Yet he is very un-Godlike. Angrily, with hot word, he *smites* the rock. Once smiting was God's plan; then the quiet word ever after. How many a time has the once smitten Rock been smitten again in our impatience! *The waters came!* Just like God! They were cared for, though He had been disobeyed and dishonoured. And there are the crowds eagerly drinking with faces down; and up yonder in the shadow standeth God *grieved,* deeply grieved at the false picture this immature people had gotten of Him that day through Moses. Moses' hot tongue and flashing eye made a deep moral scar upon their minds, that it would take years to remove. Something must be done for the people's sake. Moses disobeyed God. He dishonoured God. Yet the waters came, for *they needed water.* And God is ever tender-hearted. But they must be taught the need of obedience, the evil of disobedience. Taught it so they never could forget.

Moses was a leader. Leaders may not do as common men. And leaders may not be dealt with as followers. They stand too high in the air. They affect too many lives. So God said to Moses:—"You will not go to Canaan. You may lead them clear up to the line; you may even see over, but you may not go in." That hurt Moses deep down. It hurt God deeper down, in a heart more sensitive to hurt than was Moses'. Without doubt it was said with *reluctance,* for *Moses'* sake. But *it was said,* plainly, irrevocably, for *their* sakes. Moses' petition was for a reversal of this decision. Once and again he asked. He wanted to see that wondrous land of God's choosing. He felt the sting too. The edge of the knife of discipline cut keenly, and the blood spurted. But God said:—"Do not speak to Me again of this." The decision was not to be changed. For Moses' sake only He would gladly have changed, judging by His previous conduct. For the sake of the nation—aye, for the sake of the prodigal world to be won back through this nation, the petiion might not be granted. That ungranted petition taught those millions the lesson of obedience, of reverence, as no command, or smoking mount, or drowning Egyptians had done. It became common talk in every tent, by every camp-fire of the tented nation. "Moses disobeyed,—he failed to reverence God;—he cannot enter Canaan."—With hushed tones, and awed hearts and moved, strangely moved facts it passed from lip to lip. Some of the women and children wept. They all loved Moses. They revered him. How gladly they would have had him go over. The double-sided truth—obedience—disobedience—kept burning in through the years.

In after years many a Hebrew mother told her baby, eager for a story, of Moses their great leader; his appearance, deep-set eyes, long beard, majestic mien, yet infinite tenderness and gentleness, the softness of strength; his presence with God in the mount, the shining face. And the baby would listen so quietly, and then the eyes would grow so big and the hush of spirit come as the mother would repeat softly, "but he could not come over into the land of promise because *he did not obey God.*" And strong fathers reminded their growing sons. And so it was woven into the warp and woof of the nation—*obedience, reverent obedience to God.* And one can well understand Moses looking down from above with grateful heart that he had been denied for *their* sakes. The unselfishness and wisdom of later years would not have made the prayer. *The prayer of a man was denied that a nation might be taught obedience.*

That More Might be Given and Gotten.

Now let us look a bit at the second of these, the portrait of Hannah the Hebrew woman. First the broader lines for perspective. This peculiar Hebrew nation had two deep dips down morally between Egypt and Babylon; between the first making, and the final breaking. The national tide ebbed very low twice, before it finally ran out in the Euphrates Valley. Elijah stemmed the tide the second time, and saved the day for a later night. The Hannah story belongs in the first of these ebb-tides; the first bad sag; the first deep gap.

The giant lawgiver is long gone. His successor, only a less giant than himself is gone too, and all that generation, and more. The giants gave way to smaller-sized leaders. Now they are gone also. The mountain peaks have been lost in the foothills, and these have yielded to dunes, and levels; mostly levels; dead levels. These mountains must have had long legs. The foothills are so far away, and are running all to toes. Now the toes have disappeared.

It is a leaderless people, for the true Leader as originally planned has been, first ignored, then forgot. The people have no ideals. They grub in the earth content. There is a deep, hidden-away current of good. But it needs leadership to bring it to the surface. A leaderless people! This is the niche of the Hannah story.

The nation was rapidly drifting down to the moral level of the lowest. At Shiloh the formal worship was kept up, but the very priests were tainted with the worst impurity. A sort of sleepy, slovenly anarchy prevailed. Every man did that which was right in his own eyes, with every indication of a gutter standard. "There was none in the land possessing power of restraint that might put them to shame in anything." No government; no dominant spirit. Indeed the actual conditions of Sodom and her sister cities of the plain existed among the people. This is the setting of the simple graphic incident of Hannah. One must get the picture clearly in mind to understand the story.

Up in the hill country of Ephraim there lived a wise-hearted religious man, a farmer, raising stock, and grain; and fruit, too, likely. He was earnest but not of the sort to rise above the habit of his time. His farm was not far from Shiloh, the national place of worship, and he made yearly trips there with the family. But the woman-degrading curse of Lamech was over his home. He had two wives. Hannah was the loved one. (No man ever yet gave his heart to two women.) She was a gentle-spoken, thoughtful woman, with a deep, earnest spirit. But she had a disppointment which grew in intensity as it continued. The desire of her heart had been withheld. She was childless.

Though the thing is not mentioned the whole inference is that she prayed earnestly and persistently but to her surprise and deep disappointment the desired answer came not. To make it worse her rival—what a word, for the other one in the home with her—her rival provoked her sore to make her fret.

And that thing *went on* year after year. That teasing, nagging, picking of a small nature was her constant prod. What an atmosphere for a home! Is it any wonder that "she was in bitterness of soul" and "wept sore"? Her husband tenderly tries to comfort her. But her inner spirit remains chafed to the quick. And all this goes on for years; the yearning, the praying, the failure of answer, the biting, bitter atmosphere,—for *years*. And she wonders why.

Why was it? Step back and up a bit and get the broader view which the narrow limits of her surroundings, and shall I say, too, though not critically, of her spirit, shut out from her eyes. Here is what she saw: her fondest hope unrealized, long praying unanswered, a constant ferment at home. Here is what she wanted:—*a son*. That is her horizon. Beyond that her thought does not rise.

Here is what God saw:—a nation—no, much worse—*the* nation, in which centred His great love-plan for winning His prodigal world, going to pieces. The messenger to the prodigal was being slyly, subtly seduced by the prodigal. The saviour-nation was being itself lost. The plan so long and patiently fostered for saving a world was threatened with utter disaster.

Here is what He wanted—*a leader!* But there were no leaders. And, worse yet, there were no men out of whom leaders might be made, no men of leader-size. And worse yet *there were no women* of the sort to train and shape a man for leadership. That is the lowest level to which a people ever gets, aye, ever *can* get. God had to get a woman before He could get a man. Hannah had in her the making of the woman He needed. God honoured her by choosing her. But she must be changed before she could be used. And so there came those years of pruning, and sifting, and discipline. Shall we spell that word discipline with a final g instead of e—discipling, so the love of it may be plainer to our nearsightedness? And out of those years and experiences there came a new woman. A woman with vision broadened, with spirit mellowed, with strength seasoned, with will so sinewy supple as to yield to a higher will, to sacrifice the dearest *personal pleasure* for the world-wide purpose; willing that he who was her dearest treasure should be the nation's *first*.

Then followed months of prayer while the man was coming. Samuel was born, no, farther back yet, was conceived in the atmosphere of prayer and devotion to God. The prenatal influences for those months gave the sort of man God wanted. And a nation, *the* nation, the *world-plan,* was saved! This man became a living answer to prayer. The romantic story of the little boy up in the Shiloh tabernacle quickly spread over the nation. His very name—Samuel, God hears—sifted into people's ears the facts of a God, and of the power of prayer. The very sight of the boy and of the man clear to the end kept deepening the brain impression through eyeballs that God answers prayer. And the seeds of that re-belief in God that Samuel's leadership brought about were sown by the unusual story of his birth.

The answer was delayed that more might be given and gotten. And Hannah's exultant song of praise reveals the fineness to which the texture of her nature had been spun. And it tells too how grateful she was for a God who in great patience and of strong deliberate purpose delayed the answer to her prayer.

The Best Light for Studying a Thorn.

The third great picture in this group is that of Paul and his needle-pointed thorn. Talks about the certainty of prayer being answered are very apt to bring this question: "What about Paul's thorn?" Sometimes asked by earnest hearts puzzled; *some*times with a look in the eye almost exultant as though of gladness for that thorn because it seems to help out a theory. These pictures are put into the gallery for our help. Let us pull up our chairs in front of this one and see what points we may get to help our hearts.

First a look at Paul himself. The best light on this thorn is through the man. The man explains the thorn. We have a halo about Paul's head; and rightly, too. What a splendid man of God he was! God's chosen one for a peculiar ministry. One of the twelve could be used to open the door to the great outside world, but God had to go aside from this circle and get a man of different training for this wider sphere. Cradled and schooled in a Jewish atmosphere, he never lost the Jew standpont, yet the training of his home surroundings in that outside world, the contact with Greek culture, his natural mental cast fitted him peculiarly for his appointed task to the great outside majority. His keen reasoning powers, his vivid imagination, his steel-like will, his burning devotion, his unmovable purpose, his tender attachment to his Lord,—what a man! Well might the Master want to win such a man for service' sake. But Paul had some weak traits. Let us say it very softly, remembering as we instinctively will, that where we think of one in him there come crowding to memory's door many more in one's self. A man's weak point is usually the extreme opposite swing of the pendulum on his strong point. Paul had a tremendous will. He was a giant, a Hercules in his will. Those tireless journeys with their terrific experiences, all spell out *will* large and black. But, gently now, he went to extremes here. Was it due to his overtired nerves? Likely enough. He was obstinate, *sometimes;* stubborn; set in his way: *sometimes* head down, jaw locked, driving hard. Say it all *softly,* for we are speaking of dear old saintly Paul; but, to help, *say* it, for it is true.

God had a hard time holding Paul to *His* plans. Paul had some of his own. We can all easily understand that. Take a side glance or two as he is pushing eagerly, splendidly on. Turn to that sixteenth chapter of Acts,[1] and listen: "Having

[1]Acts 16:6

been forbidden of the Holy Spirit to speak the world in (the province of) Asia," coupled with the fact of sickness being allowed to overtake him in Galatia where the "forbidding" message came. And again this, "they assayed to go into Bithynia; and the Spirit of Jesus suffered them not."[1] Tell me, is this the way the Spirit of God leads? That I should go driving ahead until He must pull me up with a sharp turn, and twist me around! It is the way He is obliged to do many times, no doubt, with most of us. But His Chosen way? His own way? Surely not. Rather this, the keeping close, and quiet and listening for the next step. Rather the "I go not up yet unto this feast" of Jesus.[2] And then in a few days going up, evidently when the clear intimation came. These words, "assayed to go," "forbidden," "suffered not"—what flashlights they let into this strong man's character.

But there is much stronger evidence yet. Paul had an ambition to preach to the *Jerusalem Jews*. It burned in his bones from the early hours of his new life. The substratum of *"Jerusalem"* seemed ever in his thoughts and dreams. If *he* could just get to those Jerusalem Jews! He knew them. He had trained with them. He was a leader among the younger set. When they burned against these Christians he burned just a bit hotter. They knew him. They trusted him to drive the opposite wedge. If only *he* could have a chance down there he felt that the tide might be turned. But from that critical hour on the Damascene road *"Gentiles—Gentiles"* had been sounded in his ears. And he obeyed, of course he obeyed, with all his ardent heart. *But, but*—those *Jerusalem Jews! If* he might go to Jerusalem! Yet very early the Master had proscribed the Jerusalem service for Paul. He made it a matter of a special vision,[3] in the holy temple, kindly explaining why. "They will not receive of *thee* testimony concerning Me." Would that not seem quite sufficient? Surely. Yet this astoni-

---

[1] Acts 16:7.   [2] John 7:8.   [3] Acts 22:17-21.

shing thing occurs:—Paul attempts to argue with the Master *why* he should be allowed to go. This is going to great lengths; a subordinate arguing with his commanding general after the orders have been issued! The Master closes the vision with a peremptory word of command, "*depart.* I will send thee *far hence* (from Jerusalem, where you long to be), to the Gentiles." That is a picture of this man. It reveals the weak side in this giant of strength and of love. And *this* is the man God has to use in His plan. He is without doubt the best man available. And in his splendour he stands head and shoulders above his generation and many generations. Yet (with much reverence) God has a hard time getting Paul to work always along the line of *His* plans.

That is the man. Now for the thorn. Something came into Paul's life that was a constant irritation. He calls it a thorn. What a graphic world! A sharp point prodding into his flesh, ever prodding, sticking, sticking in; asleep, awake, stitching tent canvas, preaching, writing, that thing ever cutting its point into his sensitive flesh. Ugh! It did not disturb him so much at first, because *there was God* to go to. He went to God and said, "*Please* take this away." But it stayed and stuck. A second time the prayer; a bit more urgent; the thing sticks so. The time test is the hardest test of all. Still no change. Then praying the third time with what earnestness one can well imagine.

Now note three things: First, *There was an answer.* God answered *the man.* Though He did not grant the petition, He answered the man. He did not ignore him nor his request. Then God told Paul frankly that it was not best to take the thorn away. It was in the lonely vigil of a sleepless night, likely as not, that the wondrous Jesus-Spirit drew near to Paul. Inaudibly to outer ear but very plainly to his inner ear, He spoke in tones modulated into tender softness as of dearest friend talking with dear friend. "Paul," the voice said, "I know about that thorn—and how it hurts—it hurts Me, too.

For *your* sake, I would quickly, so quickly remove it. But—Paul"—and the voice becomes still softer—"it is a bit better for *others'* sake that it remain: the plan in My heart *through you* for thousands, yes, unnumbered thousands, Paul, can so best be worked out." That was the first part of what He said. And Paul lies thinking with a deep tinge of awe over his spirit. Then after a bit in yet quieter voice He went on to say, "I will be so close to your side; you shall have such revelations of My glory that the pain will be clear overlapped, Paul; the glory shall outstrip the eating thorn point."

I can see old Paul one night in his own hired house in Rome. It is late, after a busy day; the auditors have all gone. He is sitting on an old bench, slowing down before seeking sleep. One arm is around Luke, dear faithful Doctor Luke, and the other around young Timothy, not quite so young now. And with eyes that glisten, and utterance tremulous with emotion he is just saying:—"And dear old friends, do you know, I would not have missed this thorn, for the wondrous glory"—and his heart gets into his voice, there is a touch of the hoarseness of deep emotion, and a quavering of tone, so he waits a moment—"the wondrous *glory-presence of Jesus* that came with it."

And so out of the experience came a double blessing. There was a much fuller working of God's plan for His poor befooled world. And there was an unspeakable nearness of intimacy with his Lord for Paul. *The man was answered and the petition denied that the larger plan of service might be carried out.*

Shaping a Prayer on the Anvil of the Knees.

The last of these pictures is like Raphael's Sistine Madonna in the Dresden gallery; it is in a room by itself. One enters with a holy hush over his spirit, and, with awe in his eyes, looks at *Jesus in Gethsemane*. There is the Kidron brook, the gentle rise of ground, the grove of gnarled knotty old olive trees. The moon above is at the full. Its brightness makes these shadowed recesses the darker; blackly dark. Here is a group of men lying on the ground apparently asleep. Over yonder deeper in among the trees a smaller group reclines motionless. They, too, sleep. And, look, farther in yet is that lone figure; all alone; never more alone; save once—on the morrow.

There is a foreshadowing of this Gethsemane experience in the requested interview of the Greeks just a few intense days before. In the vision which the Greeks unconsciously brought the agony of the olive grove began. The climax is among these moon-shadowed trees. How sympathetic those inky black shadows! It takes bright light to make black shadows. Yet they were not black enough. Intense men can get so absorbed in the shadows as to forget the light.

This great Jesus! Son of God: God the Son. The Son of Man: God—a man! No draughtsman's pencil ever drew the line between His divinity and humanity; nor ever shall. For the union of divine and human is itself divine, and therefore clear beyond human ken. Here His humanity stands out, pathetically, luminously stands out. Let us speak of it very softly and think with the touch of awe deepening for this is holiest ground. The battle of the morrow is being fought out here. Calvary is in Gethsemane. The victory of the hill is won in the grove.

It is sheer impossible for man with sin grained into his fibre through centuries to understand the horror with which a sinless one thinks of actual contact with sin. As Jesus enters the grove that night it comes in upon His spirit with terrific intensity that He is actually coming into contact—with a meaning quite beyond us—coming into contact with sin. In some way all too deep for definition He is to be "made sin."[1] The language used to describe His emotions is so strong that

[1] 2 Cor. 5:21.

no adequate English words seem available for its full expression. An indescribable horror, a chill of terror, a frenzy of fright seizes Him. The poisonous miasma of sin seems to be filling His nostrils and to be stifling Him. And yonder alone among the trees the agony is upon Him. The extreme grips Him. May there not yet possibly be some other way rather than *this—this!* A bit of that prayer comes to us in tones strangely altered by deepest emotion. *"If it be possible—let this cup pass."* There is still a clinging to a possibility, some possibility other than that of this nightmare vision. The writer of the Hebrews lets in light here. The strain of spirit almost snaps the life-thread. And a parenthetical prayer for strength goes up. And the angels come with sympathetic strengthening. With what awe must they have ministered! Even after that some of the red life slips out there under the trees. By and by a calmer mood asserts itself, and out of the darkness a second petition comes. It tells of the tide's turning, and the victory full and complete. *A changed petition* this! *"Since this cup may not pass*—since only thus *can* Thy great plan for a world be wrought out—*Thy—will"*—slowly but very distinctly the words come—*"Thy—will—be—done."*

The changed prayer was wrought out upon His knees! With greatest reverence, and a hush in our voices, let us say that there alone with the Father came the clearer understanding of the Father's actual will under these circumstances.

> "Into the woods my Master went
> Clean forspent, forspent;
> Into the woods my Master came
> Forspent with love and shame.
> But the olives they were not blind to Him,
> The little gray leaves were kind to Him,
> The thorn-tree had a mind to Him,
> When into the woods He came.

"Out of the woods my Master went
    And He was well content;
Out of the woods my Master came
    Content with death and shame.
When death and shame would woo Him last
From under the trees they drew Him last
'Twas on a tree they slew Him—last
When out of the woods He came."[1]

True prayer is wrought out upon the knees alone with God. With deepest reverence, and in awed tones, let it be said, that *that was true of Jesus* in the days of His humanity. How infinitely more of us!

Shall we not plan to meet God alone, habitually, with the door shut, and the Book open, and the will pliant so we may be trained for this holy partnership of prayer. Then will come the clearer vision, the broader purpose, the truer wisdom, the real unselfishness, the simplicity of claiming and expecting, the delights of fellowship in service with Him; then too will come great victories for God in His world. Although we shall not begin to know by direct knowledge a tithe of the story until the night be gone and the dawning break and the ink-black shadows that now stain the earth shall be chased away by the brightness of His presence.

[1]Sidney Lanier.

The Traitor Prince.

There remains yet a word to be said about hindrances. It is a most important word; indeed the climactic word. What has been said is simply clearing the way for what is yet to be said. A very strange phase of prayer must be considered here. Strange only because not familiar. Yet though strange it contains the whole heart of the question. Here lies the fight of the fight. One marvels that so little is said of it. For if there were clear understanding here, and then faithful practicing, there would be mightier defeats and victories: defeats for the foe; victories for our rightful prince, Jesus.

The intense fact is this: *Satan has the power to hold the answer back—for awhile; to delay the result—for a time.* He has not the power to hold it back finally, *if* some one understands and prays with quiet, steady persistence. The real pitch of prayer therefore is Satanward.

Our generation has pretty much left this individual Satan out. It is partly excusable perhaps. The conceptions of Satan and his hosts and surroundings made classical by such as Dante and Milton and Dore have done much to befog the air. Almost universally they have been taken literally whether so meant or not. One familiar with Satan's characteristics can easily imagine his cunning finger in that. He is willing even to be caricatured, or to be left out of reckoning, if so he may tighten his grip.

These suggestions of horns and hoofs, of forked tail and all the rest of it seek to give material form to this being. They are grotesque to an extreme, and therefore caricatures. A caricature so disproportions and exaggerates as to make hideous or ridiculous. In our day when every foundation of knowledge is being examined there has been a natural but unthinking turning away from the very being of Satan through these representations of him. Yet where there is a caricature there must be a true. To revolt from the true, hidden by a caricature, in revolting from the caricature is easy, but is certainly bad. It is always bad to have the truth hid from our eyes.

It is refreshing and fascinating to turn from these classical caricatures to the scriptural conception of Satan. In this Book he is a being of great beauty of person, of great dignity of position even yet, endowed with most remarkable intellectual powers, a prince, at the head of a most remarkable, compact organization which he has wielded with phenomenal skill and success in furthering his ambitious purposes.

And he is not chained yet. I remember a conversation with a young clergyman on Monday morning in the reading-room of a Young Men's Christian Association. It was in a certain mining town in the southwest, which is as full of evil resorts as such places usually are. The day before, Sunday, had been one of special services, and we had both been busy and were a bit weary. We were slowing down and chatting leisurely. I remarked to my friend, "What a glad day it will be when the millennium comes!" He quickly replied, "I think this is the millennium." "But," I said, "I thought Satan was to be chained during that time. Doesn't it say something of that sort in the Book?" "Yes," he replied, "it does. But I think he is chained now." And I could not resist the answer that came blurting its way out, "Well, if he is chained, he must have a fairly long chain: it seems to permit much freedom of action." From all that can be gathered regarding this mighty prince he is not chained yet. We would do well to learn more about him. The old military maxim, "Study the enemy," should be followed more closely here.

It is striking that the oldest of the Bible books, and the latest, Job and Revelation, the first word and the last, give such definite information concerning him. These coupled with the gospel records supply most of the information available though not all. Those three and a half years of Jesus' public work is the period of greatest Satanic and

demoniac activity of which any record has been made. Jesus'
own allusions to him are frequent and in unmistakable
language. There are four particular passages to which I want
to turn your attention now. Let it not be supposed, however,
that this phase of prayer rests upon a few isolated passages.
Such a serious truth does not hinge upon selected proof texts.
It is woven into the very texture of this Book throughout.

There are two facts that run through the Bible from one
end to the other. They are like two threads ever crossing in
the warp and woof of a finely woven fabric. Anywhere you
run your shears into the web of this Book you will fine these
two threads. They run crosswise and are woven inextricably
in. One is a black thread, inky black, pot-black. The other is
a bright thread, like a bit of glory light streaming across.
These two threads everywhere. The one is this—the black
thread—there is an enemy. Turn where you will from Genesis
to Revelation—always an enemy. He is keen. He is subtle. He
is malicious. He is cruel. He is obstinate. He is a master. The
second thread is this: the leaders for God have always been
men of prayer above everything else. They are men of power
in other ways, preachers, men of action, with power to sway
others but above all else men of prayer. They give prayer first
place. There is one striking exception to this, namely, King
Soul. And most significantly a study of this exception throws
a brilliant lime light upon the career of Satan. King Saul
seems to furnish the one great human illustration in scripture
of heaven's renegade fallen prince. These special paragraphs
to be quoted are like the pattern in the cloth where the colours of the yarn come into more definite shape. The gospels
form the central pattern of the whole where the colours pile
up into sharpest contrast.

Praying is Fighting.

But let us turn to the Book at once. For we *know* only what
it tells. The rest is surmise. The only authoritative statements

about Satan seem to be these here. Turn first to the New Testament.

The Old Testament is the book of illustrations; the New of explanations, of teaching. In the Old, teaching is largely by kindergarten methods. The best methods, for the world was in its child stage. In the New the teaching is by precept. There is precept teaching in the Old; very much. There is picture teaching in the New; the gospels full of it. But picture teaching, acted teaching, is the characteristic of the Old, and precept teaching of the New. There is a wonderfully vivid picture in the Old Testament, of this thing we are discussing. But first let us get the teaching counterpart in the new, and then look at the picture.

Turn to Ephesians. Ephesians is a prayer epistle. That is a very significant fact to mark. Of Paul's thirteen letters Ephesians is peculiarly the prayer letter. Paul is clearly in a prayer mood. He is on his knees here. He has much to say to these people whom he has won to Christ, but it comes in the parentheses of his prayer. The connecting phrase running through is—"for this cause I pray...I bow my knees." Half-way through this rare old man's mind runs out to the condition of these churches, and he puts in the always needed practical injunctions about their daily lives. Then the prayer mood reasserts itself, and the epistle finds its climax in a remarkable paragraph on prayer. The climax of this prayer-epistle is this paragraph and the climax of this paragraph is prayer. From praying the man goes to urging them to pray.

We must keep the book open here as we talk: chapter six, verses ten to twenty inclusive. The main drive of all their living and warfare seems very clear to this scarred veteran: —"that ye may be able to withstand the wiles of the devil." This man seems to have had no difficulty in believing in a personal devil. Probably he had had too many close encounters for that. To Paul Satan is a cunning strategist requiring every bit of available resource to combat.

This paragraph states two things:—who the real foe is, against whom the fight is directed; and, then with climactic intensity it pitches on the main thing that routs him. Who is the real foe? Listen:—"For our wrestling is not against flesh and blood"—not against men; never that; something far subtler—"but against the principalities"—a word for a compact organization of individuals,—"against powers"—not only organized but highly endowed intellectually, "against the world-rulers of this darkness," —they are of princely kin; not common folk—"against the hosts of wicked spirits in the heavenlies"—spirit beings, in vast numbers, having their headquarters somewhere above the earth. *That* is the foe. Large numbers of highly endowed spirit beings, compactly organized, who are the sovereigns of the present realm or age of moral darkness, have their *headquarters* of activity somewhere above the earth, and below the throne of God, but concerned with human beings upon the earth. In chapter two of the epistle the head or ruler of this organization is referred to, "the prince of the powers of the air."[1] That is the real foe.

Then in one of his strong piled up climactic sentences Paul tells how the fight is to be won. This sentence runs unbroken through verses fourteen to twenty inclusive. There are six preliminary clauses in it leading up to its main statement. These clauses name the pieces of armour used by a Roman soldier in the action of battle. The loins girt, the breastplate on, the feet shod, the shield, the helmet, the sword, and so on. A Roman soldier reading this or, hearing Paul preach it, would expect him to finish the sentence by saying *"with all your fighting strength fighting."*

That would be the proper conclusion rhetorically of this sentence. But when Paul reaches the climax with his usual intensity he drops the rhetorical figure, and puts in the thing

---

[1] Ephesians 2:2.

with which in our case the fighting is done—"with all prayer *praying.*" In place of the expected word fighting is the word praying. The thing with which the fighting is done is put in place of the word itself. Our fighting is praying. Praying is fighting, spirit-fighting. That is to say, this old evangelist-missionary-bishop says, we are in the thick of a fight. There is a war on. How shall we best fight? First get into good shape to pray, and then with all your praying strength and skill *pray.* That word *praying* is the climax of this long sentence, and of this whole epistle. This is the sort of action that turns the enemy's flank, and reveals his heels. He simply *cannot* stand before persistent knee-work.

Now mark the keenness of Paul's description of the man who does most effective work in praying. These are six qualifications under the figure of the six pieces of armour. A clear understanding of truth, a clean obedient life, earnest service, a strongly simple trust in God, clear assurance of one's own salvation and relation to God, and a good grip of the truth for others—these things prepare a man for the real conflict of prayer. *Such a man—praying—drives back these hosts of the traitor prince.* Such a man praying is invincible in his Chief, Jesus. The equipment is simple, and in its beginnings comes quickly to the willing, earnest heart.

Look a bit at how the strong climax of this long sentence runs. It is fairly bristling with points. Soldier-points all of them; like bayonet points. Just such as a general engaged in a siegefight would give to his men. "With all prayer and supplication"—there is *intensity;* "praying"—that is *the main drive;* "at all seasons"—*ceaselessness,* night and day; hot and cold; wet and dry; "in the Spirit"—as *guided by the Chief;* "and watching thereunto"—*sleepless vigilance;* watching is ever a fighting word; watch the enemy; watch your own forces; "with all perseverance"—*persistence;* cheery, jaw-locked, dogged persistence, bulldog tenacity; "and supplication"—*intensity again;* "for all the saints"—*the sweep of the action,* keep in touch with the whole army; "and on my behalf"—the human leader, rally around *the immediate leader.* This is the foe to be fought. And this the sort of fighting that defeats this foe.

A Double Wrestling Match.

Now turn back to the illustration section of our Book for a remarkably graphic illustration of these words. It is in the old prophecy of Daniel, tenth chapter. The story is this: Daniel is an old man now. He is an exile. He has not seen the green hills of his fatherland since boyhood. In this level Babylon, he is homesick for the dear old Palestinian hills, and he is heartsick over the plight of his people. He has been studying Jeremiah's prophecies, and finds there the promise plainly made that after seventy years these exiled Hebrews are to be allowed to return. Go back again! The thought of it quickens his pulsebeats. He does some quick counting. The time will soon be up. So Daniel plans a bit of time for special prayer, a sort of siege prayer.

Remember who he is—this Daniel. He is the chief executive of the land. He controls, under the king, the affairs of the world empire of his time. He is a giant of strength and ability—this man. But he plans his work so as to go away for a time. Taking a few kindred spirits, who understand prayer, he goes off into the woods down by the great Tigris River. They spend a day in fasting, and meditation and prayer. Not utter fasting, but scant eating of plain food. I suppose they pray awhile; maybe separately, then together; then read a bit from the Jeremiah parchment, think and talk it over and then pray some more. And so they spend a whole day reading, meditating, praying.

They are expecting an answer. These oldtime intercessors were strong in expectancy. But there is no answer. A second day, a third, a fourth, a week, still no answer reaches them. They go quietly on without hesitation. Two weeks. How long it must have seemed! Think of fourteen days spent *waiting;* waiting for something, with your heart on tenter hooks. There is no answer. God might have been dead, to adapt the words of Catharine Luther, so far as any answer reaching them is concerned. But you cannot befool Daniel in that way. He is an old hand at prayer. Apparently he has no thought of quitting. He goes quietly, steadily on. Twenty days pass, with no change. Still they persist. Then the twenty-first day comes and there is an answer. It comes in a vision whose glory is beyond human strength to bear. By and by when they can talk, his visitor and he, this is what Daniel hears: "Daniel, the first day you began to pray, your prayer was heard, and I was sent with the answer." And even Daniel's eyes open big—"the *first* day—three weeks ago?" "Yes, three weeks ago I left the presence of God with the answer to your prayer. But"—listen, here is the strange part—"the prince of the kingdom of Persia withstood me, resisted me, one and twenty days: but Michael, your prince, came to help me, and I was free to come to you with the answer to your prayer."

Please notice four things that I think any one reading this chapter will readily admit. This being talking with Daniel is plainly a spirit being. He is opposed by some one. This opponent plainly must be a spirit being, too, to be resisting a spirit being. Daniel's messenger is from God: that is clear. Then the opponent must be from the opposite camp. And here comes in the thing strange, unexpected, the evil spirit being *has the power to detain, hold back God's messenger* for three full weeks by earth's reckoning of time. Then reenforcements come, as we would say. The evil messenger's purpose is defeated, and God's messenger is free to come as originally planned.

There is a double scene being enacted. A scene you can see, and a scene you cannot see. An unseen wrestling match in the upper spirit realm, and two embodied spirit beings down on their faces by the river. And both concerned over the same thing.

That is the Daniel story. What an acted out illustration it is of Paul's words. It is a picture glowing with the action of real life. It is a double picture. Every prayer action is in doubles; a lower human level; an upper spirit level. Many see only the seen, and lose heart. While we look at the things that are seen, let us gaze intently at the things unseen; for the seen things are secondary, but the unseen are chief, and the action of life is being decided there.

Here is the lower, the seen;—a group of men, led by a man of executive force enough to control an empire, prone on their faces, with minds clear, quiet, alert, persistently, ceaselessly *praying* day by day. Here is the upper, the unseen:—a "wrestling," keen, stubborn, skilled, going on between two spirit princes in the spirit realm. And by Paul's explanation the two are vitally connected. Daniel and his companions are wrestlers too, active participants in that upper-air fight, and really deciding the issue, for they are on the ground being contested. These men are indeed praying with all prayer and supplication at all times, in the Spirit, and watching thereunto with all perseverance and supplication, and *at length victory comes.*

Prayer Concerns Three.

Now a bit of a look at the central figure of the pattern. Jesus lets in a flood of light on Satan's relation to prayer in one of His prayer parables. There are two parables dealing distinctively with prayer: "the friend at midnight,"[1] and "the unjust judge."[2] The second of these deals directly with this Satan phase of prayer. It is Luke through whom we learn most of Jesus' own praying who preserves for us this remarkable prayer picture.

It comes along towards the end. The swing has been made

from plain talking to the less direct, parable-form of teaching. The issue with the national leaders has reached its acutest stage. The culmination of their hatred, short of the cross, found vent in charging Him with being inspired by the spirit of Satan. He felt their charge keenly and answered it directly and fully. His parable of the strong man being bound before his house can be rifled comes in here. *They* had no question as to what that meant. That is the setting of this prayer parable. The setting is a partial interpretation. Let us look at this parable rather closely, for it is full of help for those who would become skilled in helping God win His world back home again.

Jesus seems so eager that they shall not miss the meaning here that He departs from His usual habit and says plainly what this parable is meant to teach:—"that men ought always to pray, and not to faint." The great essential, He says, is *prayer*. The great essential in prayer is *persistence*. The temptation in prayer is that one may lose heart, and give up, or give in. "Not-to-faint" tells how keen the contest is.

There are three persons in the parable; a judge, a widow, and an adversary. The judge is utterly selfish, unjust, godless, and reckless of anybody's opinion. The worst sort of man, indeed, the last sort of man to be a judge. Inferentially he knows that the right of the case before him is with the widow. The widow—well, she is a *widow*. Can more be said to make the thing vivid and pathetic! A very picture of friendlessness and helplessness is a widow. A woman needs a friend. This woman has lost her nearest, dearest friend; her protector. She is alone. There is an adversary, an opponent at law, who has unrighteously or illegally gotten an advantage over the widow and is ruthlessly pushing her to the wall. She is seeking to get the judge to join with her against her adversary. Her urgent, oft repeated request is, "avenge me of mine adversary." That is Jesus' pictorial illustration of persistent prayer.

Let us look into a little further. "Adversary" is a common

word in scripture for Satan. He is the accuser, the hater, the
enemy, the adversary. Its meaning technically is "an opponent in a suit at law." It is the same word as used later by
Peter, "Your adversary the devil as a roaring lion, goeth
about, seeking whom he may devour."[1] The word "avenge"
used four times really means, "do me justice." It suggests
that the widow has the facts on her side to win a clear case,
and that the adversary has been bully-ragging his case
through by sheer force.

There is a strange feature to this parable, which must have
a meaning. *An utterly godless unscrupulous man is put in to
represent God!* This is startling. In any other than Jesus it
would seem an overstepping of the bounds. But there is keenness of a rare sort here. Such a man is chosen for judge to
bring out most sharply this:—the sort of thing required to
win this judge is certainly not required *with God*. The widow
must persist and plead because of the sort of man she has to
deal with. But God is utterly different in character. Therefore
while persistence is urged in prayer plainly it is not for the
reason that required the widow to persist. And if that reason
be cut out it leaves only one other, namely, that represented
by the adversary.

Having purposely put such a man in the parable for God,
Jesus takes pains to speak of the real character of God. "And
He is *long-suffering* over them." *That* is God. That word
"long-suffering" and its equivalent on Jesus' lips suggests at
once the strong side of love, namely, *patience,* gentle, fine patience. It has bothered the scholars in this phrase to know
with whom or over what the long-suffering is exercised.
"Over them" is the doubtful phrase. Long-suffering over
these praying ones? *Or,* long-suffering in dealing righteously
with some stubborn adversary—which? The next sentence
has a word set in sharpest contrast with this one, namely

[1] 1 Peter 5:8.

"speedily." "Long-suffering" yet "speedily."

Here are gleams of bright light on a dark subject with apparently more light obscured than is allowed to shine through. Jesus always spoke thoughtfully. He chooses His words. Remembering the adversary against whom the persistence is directed the whole story seems to suggest this: that there is *a great conflict on* in the upper spirit world. Concerning it our patient God is long-suffering. He is a just and righteous God. These beings in the conflict are all His creatures. He is just in His dealings with the devil and his splendid host of evil spirits even as with all His creation. He is long-suffering that no unfairness shall be done in His dealings with these creatures of His. Yet at the same time He is doing His best to bring the conflict to a speedy end, for the sake of His loyal loved ones, and that right may prevail.

The upshot of the parable is very plain. It contains for us two tremendous, intense truths. First is this: *prayer concerns three,* not two but three. God to whom we pray, the man on the contested earth who prays, and the evil one against whom we pray. And the purpose of the prayer is not to persuade or influence God, but to join forces with Him against the enemy. Not towards God, but with God against Satan—that is the main thing to keep in mind in prayer. The real pitch is not Godward but Satanward.

The second intense truth is this:—the winning quality in prayer is *persistence.* The final test is here. This is the last ditch. Many who fight well up to this point lose their grip here, and so lose all. Many who are well equipped for prayer fail here, and doubtless fail because they have not rightly understood. With clear, ringing tones the Master's voice sounds in our ears again to-day, "always to pray, *and* not to faint."

A Stubborn Foe Routed.

That is the parable teaching. Now a look at a plain out

word from the Master's lips. It is in the story of the demonized boy, the distressed father, and the defeated disciples, at the foot of the transfiguration mountain.[1] Extremes meet here surely. The mountain peak is in sharpest contrast with the valley. The demon seems to be of the superlative degree. His treatment of the possessed boy is malicious to an extreme. His purpose is "to destroy" him. Yet there is a limit to his power, for what he would do he has not yet been able to do. He shows extreme tenacity. He fought bitterly against being disembodied again. (can it be that embodiment eases in some way the torture of existence for these prodigal spirits!) And so far he fought well, and with success. The disciples had tried to cast him out. They were expected to. They expected to. They had before. They failed!—dismally—amid the sneering and jeering of the crowd and the increasing distress of the poor father.

Then Jesus came. Was some of the transfiguring glory still lingering in that great face? It would seem so. The crowd was "amazed" when they saw Him, and "saluted" Him. His presence changed all. The demon angrily left, doing his worst to wreck the house he had to vacate. The boy is restored; and the crowd astonished at the power of God.

Then these disciples did a very keen thing. They made some bad blunders but this is not one of them. They sought a private talk with Jesus. No shrewder thing was ever done. When you fail, quit your service and get away for a private interview with Jesus. With eyes big, and voices dejected, the question wrung itself out of their sinking hearts, "Why could not *we* cast it out?" Matthew and Mark together supply the full answer. Probably first came this:—"because of your little faith." They had quailed in their hearts before the power of this malicious demon. And the demon knew it. They were more impressed with the power of the demon than with the

---

[1] Matthew 17:14-20; Mark 9:14-29; Luke 9:37-43.

power of God. And the demon saw it. They had not prayed victoriously against the demon. The Master says, "faith only as big as a mustard seed (you cannot measure the strength of the mustard seed by its size) will say to this mountain—'Remove.' " Mark keenly:—the direction of the faith is towards the obstacle. Its force is against the enemy. It was the demon who was most directly influenced by Jesus' faith.

Then comes the second part of the reply:—"This kind can come out by nothing but by prayer." Some less-stubborn demons may be cast out by the faith that comes of our regular prayer-touch with God. This extreme sort takes special prayer. This kind of a demon goes out by prayer. It can be put out by nothing less. The real victory must be in the secret place. The exercise of faith in the open battle is then a mere pressing of the victory already won. These men had the language of Jesus on their lips, but they had not gotten the victory first off somewhere alone. This demon is determined not to go. He fights stubbornly and strongly. He succeeds. Then this *Man of Prayer* came. The quiet word of command is spoken. The demon must go. These disciples were strikingly like some of us. They had not *realized* where the real victory is won. They had used the word of command to the demon, doubtless coupling Jesus' name with it. But there was not the secret touch with God that gives victory. Their eyes showed their fear of the demon.

Prayer, real prayer, intelligent prayer, it is this that routs Satan's demons, for it routs their chief. David killed the lion and bear in the secret forests before he faced the giant in the open. These disciples were facing the giant in the open without the discipline in secret. "This kind can be compelled to come out by nothing but by prayer," means this:—"this kind comes out, and must come out, before the man who prays." This thing which Jesus calls prayer casts out demons. Would that we knew better by experience what He meant by prayer. It exerts a positive influence upon the hosts of evil spirits. They fear it. They fear the man who becomes skilled in its use.

There are yet many other passages in this Bible fully as explicit as these, and which give on the very surface just such plain teaching as these. The very language of scripture throughout is full of this truth. But these four great instances are quite sufficient to make the present point clear and plain. This great renegade prince is an actual active factor in the lives of men. He believes in the potency of prayer. He fears it. He can hinder its results for a while. He does his best to hinder it, and to hinder as long as possible.

Prayer overcomes him. It defeats his plans and himself. He cannot successfully stand before it. He trembles when some man of simple faith in God prays. Prayer is insistence upon God's will being done. It needs for its practice a man in sympathetic touch with God. Its basis is Jesus' victory. It overcomes the opposing will of the great traitor-leader.

III. HOW TO PRAY

The "How" of Relationship

God's Ambassadors.

If I had an ambition to be the ambassador of this country to our mother-country, there would be two essential things involved. The first and great essential would be to receive the appointment. I would need to come into certain relation with our president, to possess certain qualifications considered essential by him, and to secure from his hand the appointment, and the official credentials of my appointment. That would establish my relationship to the foreign court as the representative of my own country, and my right to transact business in her name.

But having gotten that far I might go over there and make bad mistakes. I might get our diplomatic relations tangled up, requiring many explanations, and maybe apologies, and leaving unpleasant memories for a long time to come. Such incidents have not been infrequent. Nations are very sensitive. Governmental affairs must be handled with great nicety. There would be a second thing which if I were a wise enough man to be an ambassador I would likely do. I would go to see John Hay and Joseph H. Choate, and have as many interviews with them as possible, and learn all I possible could from them of London official life, court etiquette, personages to be dealt with, things to do, and things to avoid. How to be a successful diplomat and further the good feeling between the two governments, and win friends for our country among the sturdy Britons would be my one absorbing thought. And having gotten all I could in that way I would be constantly on the alert with all the mental keenness I could command to practice being a successful ambassador.

The first of these would make me technically an ambassador. The second would tend towards giving me some skill as an ambassador. Now there are the same two how's in praying. First the relationship must be established before any business can be transacted. Then skill must be acquired in the transacting of the business on hand.

Just now, we want to talk about the first of these, the how of relationship in prayer. The basis of prayer is right relationship with God. Prayer is representing God in the spirit realm of this world. It is insisting upon His rights down in this sphere of action. It is standing for Him with full powers from Him. Clearly the only basis of such relationship to God is *Jesus.* We have been outlawed by sin. We were in touch with God. We broke with Him. The break could not be repaired by us. Jesus came. He was God *and* Man. He touches both. We get back through Him, and only so. The blood of the cross is the basis of all prayer. Through it the relationship is established that underlies all prayer. Only as I come to God through Jesus to get the sin score straightened, and only as I keep in sympathy with Jesus in the purpose of my life can I practice prayer.

Six Sweeping Statements.

Jesus' own words make this very clear. There are two groups of teachings on prayer in those three and a half years as given by the gospel records. The first of these groups is in the Sermon on the Mount which Jesus preached about half-way through the second year of His ministry. The second group comes sheer at end. All of it is in the last six months, and most of it in the last ten days, and much of that on the very eve of that last tragic day.

It is after the sharp rapture with the leaders that this second series of statements is made. The most positive, and most sweeping utterances on prayer are here. Of Jesus' eight promises regarding prayer six are here. I want to ask you please to notice these six promises or statements; and then, to notice their relation to our topic of to-day.

In Matthew 18:19, 20, is the first of these. "Again I say unto you, that if two of you shall agree on earth, as touching anything that they shall ask, it shall be done for them of My

Father who is in heaven." Notice the place of prayer—"on earth"; and the sweep—"anything"; and the positiveness—"it shall be done." Then the reason why is given. "For where two or three are gathered in My name, there am I in the midst of them." That is to say, if there are two persons praying, there are three. If three meet to pray, there are four praying. There is always one more than you can see. And if you might perhaps be saying to yourself in a bit of dejection, "He'll not hear me: I'm so sinful: so weak"—you would be wrong in thinking and saying so, but then we do think and say things that are not right—*if* you might be thinking that, you could at once fall back upon this: the Father always hears Jesus. And wherever earnest hearts pray Jesus is there taking their prayer and making it His prayer.

The second of these: Mark 11:22-24, "Jesus answering saith unto them, have faith in God"—with the emphasis double-lined under "God." The chief factor in prayer is God. "Verily I say unto you, whosover shall say unto this mountain, be thou taken up and cast into the sea——" Choosing, do you see the unlikeliest thing that might occur. Such a thing did not take place. We never hear of Jesus moving an actual mountain. The need for such action does not seem to have arisen. But He chooses the thing most difficult for His illustration. Can you imagine a mountain moving off into the sea—the Jungfrau, or Blanc, or Ranier? If you know mountains down in your country you cannot imagine it actually occurring. "——And shall not doubt in his heart——" That is Jesus' definition of faith. "——But shall believe that what he saith cometh to pass; he shall have it. Therefore, I say unto you, all things whatsoever ye pray and ask for, believe that ye receive them, and ye shall have them." How utterly sweeping this last statement! And to make it more positive it is preceded by the emphatic "therefore—I—say —unto—you." Both whatsoever and whosoever are here. Anything, and anybody. We always feel instinctively as though these statements need careful guarding: a few fences put up around them. Wait a bit and we shall see what the Master's own fence is.

The last four of the six are in John's gospel. In that last long quiet talk on the night in which he was betrayed. John preserves much of that heart-talk for us in chapters thirteen to seventeen.

Here in John 14:13, 14: "And whatsoever ye shall ask in My name, that will I do, that the Father may be glorified in the Son. If ye shall ask anything in My name, that will I do." The repetition is to emphasize the unlimited sweep of what may be asked.

John 15:7: "If ye abide in Me, and My words abide in you——" That word abide is a strong word. It does not mean to leave your cards; nor to hire a night's lodging; nor to pitch a tent, or run up a miner's shanty, or a lumberman's shack. It means moving in to stay. "——Ask whatsoever ye will——" The Old Version says, "ye shall ask." But here the revised is more accurate: "Ask; please ask; I ask you to ask." There is nothing said directly about God's will. There is something said about our wills. "——And it shall be done unto you." Or, a little more literally, "I will bring it to pass for you."

I remember the remark quoted to me by a friend one day. His church membership is in the Methodist Church of the North, but his service crosses church lines both in this country and abroad. He was talking with one of the bishops of that church whose heart was in the foreign mission field. The bishop was eager to have this friend serve as missionary secretary of his church. But he knew, as everybody knows, how difficult appointments oftentimes are in all large bodies. He was earnestly discussing the matter with my friend, and made this remark: "If you will allow the use of your name for this appointment, *I will lay myself out* to have it made." Now if you will kindly not think there is any lack of reverence in my saying so—and there is surely non in my thought—that is the practical meaning of Jesus' words here. "If you abide in Me, and My words sway you, you please ask what is your will to ask. And—softly, reverently now—I will lay Myself out to bring that thing to pass for you." That is the force of His words here.

This same chapter, sixteenth verse: "Ye did not choose Me, but I chose you, and appointed you, that ye should go and bear fruit, and that your fruit should abide; that whatsoever ye shall ask of the Father in My name, He may give it you." God had our prayer partnership with Himself in His mind in choosing us. And the last of these, John 16:23, 24, second clause, "Verily, verily, I say unto you, if ye shall ask anything of the Father, He will give it you in My name. Hitherto have ye asked nothing in My name: ask, and ye shall receive, that your joy may be fulfilled."

These statements are the most sweeping to be found anywhere in the Scriptures regarding prayer. There is no limitation as to who shall ask, nor the kind of thing to be asked for. There are three limitations imposed: the prayer is to be *through Jesus;* the person praying is to be in fullest sympathy with Him; and this person is to have faith.

Words With a Freshly Honed Razor-Edge.

Now please group these six sweeping statements in your mind and hold them together there. Then notice carefully this fact. These words are not spoken to the crowds. They are spoken to the small inner group of twelve disciples. Jesus talks one way to the multitude. He oftentimes talks differently to these men who have separated themselves from the crowd and come into the inner circle.

And notice further that before Jesus spoke these words to this group of men He had said something else first. Something very radical; so radical that it led to a sharp passage between Himself and Peter, to whom He speaks very sternly. This something else fixes unmistakably their relation

to Himself. Remember that the sharp break with the national
leaders has come. Jesus is charged with Satanic collusion.
The death plot is determined upon. The breach with the
leaders is past the healing point. And now the Master is frequently slipping away from the crowd with these twelve men,
and seeking to teach and train them. That is the setting of
these great promises. It must be kept continually in mind.

Before the Master gave Himself away to these men in these
promises He said this something else. It is this. I quote Matthew's account: "If any man would come after Me let him
deny himself and take up his cross (daily, Luke's addition)
and follow Me."[1] *These words should be written crosswise
over those six prayer statements.* Jesus never spoke a keener
word. Those six promises are not meant for all. Let it be said
very plainly. They are meant only for those who will square
their lives by these razor-edged words.

I may not go fully into the significance of these deep-
cutting words here. They have been gone into at some length
in a previous set of talks as suggesting the price of power. To
him whose heart burns for power in prayer I urge a careful
review of that talk in this new setting of it. "If any man
would come after Me" means a rock-rooted purpose; the jaw
locked; the tendrils of the purpose going down and around
and under the gray granite of a man's will, and trying
themselves there; and knotting the ties; sailor knots, that you
cannot undo.

"Come after Me" means all the power of Jesus' life, and
has the other side, too. It means the wilderness, the intense
temptation. It may mean the obscure village of Nazareth for
you. It may mean that first Judean year for you—lack of ap-
preciation. It may mean for you that last six months—the
desertion of those hitherto friendly. It will mean without a
doubt a Gethsemane. Everybody who comes along after

[1]Matthew 16:24.

Jesus has a Gethsemane in his life. It will never mean as much to you as it meant to Him. That is true. But, then, it will mean everything to you. And it will mean too having a Calvary in your life in a very real sense, though different from what that meant to Him. This sentence through gives the process whereby the man with sin grained into the fibre of his will may come into such relationship with God as to claim without any reservation these great prayer promises. And if that sound hard and severe to you let me quickly say that it is an easy way for the man who is *willing*. The presence of Jesus in the life overlaps every cutting thing.

If a man will go through Matthew 16:24, and habitually live there he may ask what he wills to ask, and that thing will come to pass. The reason, without question, why many people do not have power in prayer is simply because they are unwilling—I am just talking very plainly—they are unwilling to bare their breasts to the keen-edged knife in these words of Jesus. And on the other side, if a man will quietly, resolutely follow the Master's leading—nothing extreme—nothing fanatical, or morbid, just a quiet going where that inner Voice plainly leads day by day, he will be startled to find what an utterly new meaning prayer will come to have for him.

The Controlling Purpose.

Vital relationship is always expressed by purpose. The wise ambassador has an absorbing purpose to further the interests of his government. Jesus said, and it at once reveals His relationship to God, "I do always those things that are well pleasing to him."

The relationship that underlies prayer has an absorbing purpose. Its controlling purpose is to please Jesus. That sentence may sound simple enough. But, do you know, there is no sentence I might utter that has a keener, a more freshly honed razor-edge to it than that. That the purpose which *controls* my action in every matter be this: to please Him. If you have not done so, take it for a day, a week, and use it as a touch stone regarding thought, word and action. Take it into matters personal, home, business, social, fraternal. It does not mean to ask, "Is this right? is this wrong?" Nor that. Not the driving of a keen line between wrong and right. There are a great many things that can be proven to be not wrong, but that are not best, that are not His preference.

It will send a business man running his eye along the shelves and counter of his store. "The controlling purpose to please Jesus...hm-m-m, I guess maybe that stuff there ought to come out. Oh, it is not wrong: I can prove that. My Christian brother-merchants handle it here, and over the country: but *to please Him:* a good, clean sixty per cent. profit too, cash money, but *to please Him——*" and the stuff must go down and out.

It would set some women to thinking about the next time the young people are to gather in her home for a delightful social evening with her own daughters. She will think about some forms of pastime that are found everywhere. They are not wrong, that has been conclusively proven. But *to please Him.* Hm-m. And these will go out. And then it will set her to work with all her God-given woman-wit and exquisite tact to planning an evening yet more delightful. It will make one think of his personal habits, his business methods, and social intercourse, the organizations he belongs to, with the quiet question cutting it razor-way into each.

And if some one listening may ask: Why put the condition of prayer so strongly as that? I will remind you of this. The true basis of prayer is sympathy, oneness of purpose. Prayer is not extracting favours from a reluctant God. It is not passing a check in a bank window for money. That is mandatory. The roots of prayer lie down in oneness of purpose. God up yonder, His Victor-Son by His side, and a man down here, in *such sympathetic touch* that God can think His thoughts over in this man's mind, and have His desires repeated upon the earth as the man's prayer.

The Threefold Cord of Jesus' Life.

Think for a moment into Jesus' human life down here. His marvellous activities for those few years over which the world has never ceased to wonder. Then His underneath hidden-away prayer-life of which only occasional glimpses are gotten. Then grouping around about the sentence of His—"I do always the things that are pleasing to Him"—in John's gospel, pick out the emphatic negatives on Jesus' lips, the "not's": not My will, not My works, not My words. Jesus came to do somebody's else will. The controlling purpose of His life was to please His Father. That was the secret of the power of His earthly career. Right relationship to God; a secret intimate prayer-life: marvellous power over men and with men—those are the strands in the threefold cord of His life.

There is a very striking turn of a word in the second chapter of John's gospel down almost at its close. The old version says that "Many believed on His name beholding His signs which He did, but Jesus did not commit Himself unto them" because He knew them so well. The word "believed," and the word "commit" are the same word underneath our English. The sentence might run "many *trusted* Him beholding what He did; but He did not *trust* them for He knew them." I have no doubt most, or all of us here to-day, trust Him. Let me ask you very softly now: Can He trust you? While we might all shrink from saying "yes" to that, there is a very real sense in which we may say "yes," namely, in the purpose of life. Every life is controlled by some purpose. What is yours? To please Him? If so He knows it. It is a great comfort to remember that God judges a man not by his achievements, but by his purposes: not by what I am, actually, but by what I would be, in the yearning of my inmost heart, the dominant purpose of my life. God will fairly flood your life with all the power He can trust you to use wholly for Him.

Commercial practice furnishes a simple but striking illustration here. A man is employed by a business house as a clerk. His ability and honesty come to be tested in many ways constantly. He is promoted gradually, his responsibilities increased. As he proves himself thoroughly reliable he is trusted more and more, until by and by as need arises he becomes the firm's confidential clerk. He knows its secrets. He is trusted with the combination to the inner box in the vault. Because it has been proven by actual test that he will use everything only for the best interests of his house, and not selfishly.

Here, where we are dealing, the whole thing moves up to an infinitely higher level, but the principle does not change. If I will come into the relationship implied in these words:—it shall be the one controlling desire and purpose of my life to do the things that please Him—then I may ask for what I will, and it shall be done. That is how to pray: the how of relationship. The man who will live in Matthew 16:24, and follow Jesus as He leads: simply that: no fanaticism, no morbidism, no extremism, just simply follow as He leads, day by day,—then those six promises of Jesus with their wonderful sweep, their limitless sweep are his to use as he will.

Touching the Hidden Keys.

One of the most remarkable illustrations in recent times of the power of prayer, may be found in the experience of Mr. Moody. It explains his unparalleled career of world-wide soul winning. One marvels that more has not been said of it. Its stimulus to faith is great. I suppose the man most concerned did not speak of it much because of his fine modesty. The last year of his life he referred to it more frequently as though impelled to.

The last time I heard Mr. Moody was in his own church in Chicago. It was, I think, in the fall of the last year of his life. One morning in the old church made famous by his early work, in a quiet conversational way he told the story. It was back in the early seventies, when Chicago had been laid in ashes. "This building was not yet up far enough to do much in," he said; "so I thought I would slip across the water, and learn what I could from preachers there, so as to do better work here. I had gone over to London, and was running around after men there." The he told of going one evening to hear Mr. Spurgeon in the Metropolitan Tabernacle; and understanding that he was to speak a second time that evening to dedicate a chapel, Mr. Moody had slipped out of the building and had run along the street after Mr. Spurgeon's carriage a mile or so, so as to hear him the second time. Then he smiled, and said quietly, "I was running around after men like that."

He had not been speaking anywhere, he said, but listening to others. One day, Saturday, at noon, he had gone into the meeting in Exeter Hall on the Strand; felt impelled to speak a little when the meeting was thrown open, and did so. At the close among others who greeted him, one man, a minister, asked him to come and preach for him the next day morning and night, and he said he would. Mr. Moody said, "I went to the morning service and found a large church full of people.

And when the time came I began to speak to them. But it seemed the hardest talking I ever did. There was no response in their faces. They seemed as though carved out of stone or ice. And I was having a hard time: and wished I wasn't there; and wished I hadn't promised to speak again at night. But I had promised, and so I went.

"At night it was the same thing: house full, people outwardly respectful, but no interest, no response. And I was having a hard time again. When about half-way through my talk there came a change. It seemed as though the windows of heaven had opened and a bit of breath blew down. The atmosphere of the building seemed to change. The people's faces changed. It impressed me so that when I finished speaking I gave the invitation for those who wanted to be Christians to rise. I thought there might be a few. And to my immense surprise the people got up in groups, pew-fulls. I turned to the minister and said, 'What does this mean?' He said, 'I don't know, I'm sure.' Well," Mr. Moody said, "they misunderstood me. I'll explain what I meant." So he announced an aftermeeting in the room below, explaining who were invited: only those who wanted to be Christians; and putting pretty clearly what he understood that to mean, and dismissed the service.

They went to the lower room. And the people came crowding, jamming in below, filling all available space, seats, aisles and standing room. Mr. Moody talked again a few minutes, and then asked those who would be Christians to rise. This time he knew he had made his meaning clear. They god up in clumps, in groups, by fifties! Mr. Moody said, "I turned and said to the minister, 'What *does* this mean?' He said, 'I'm sure I don't know.'" Then the minister said to Mr. Moody, "What'll I do with these people? I don't know what to do with them; this is something new." And he said, "Well, I'd announce a meeting for to-morrow night, and Tuesday night, and see what comes of it; I'm going across the channel to Dublin." And he went, but he had barely stepped off the boat when a cablegram was handed him from the minister saying, "Come back at once. Church packed." So he went back, and stayed ten days. And the result of that ten days, as I recall Mr. Moody's words, was that four hundred were added to that church, and that every church near by felt the impulse of those ten days. Then Mr. Moody dropped his head, as though thinking back, and said: "I had no plans beyond this church. I supposed my life work was here. But the result with me was that I was given a roving commission and have been working under it ever since."

Now what was the explanation of that marvellous Sunday and days following? It was not Mr. Moody's doing, though he was a leader whom God could and did mightily use. It was not the minister's doing; for he was as greatly surprised as the leader. There was some secret hidden beneath the surface of those ten days. With his usual keenness Mr. Moody set himself to ferret it out.

By and by this incident came to him. A member of the church, a woman, had been taken sick some time before. Then she grew worse. Then the physician told her that she would not recover. That is, she would not die at once, so far as he could judge, but she would be shut in her home for years. And she lay there trying to think what that meant: to be shut in for years. And she thought of her life, and said, "How little I've done for God: practically nothing: and now what can I do shut in here on my back." And she said, "I can pray."

May I put this word in here as a parenthesis in the story—that God oftentimes allows us to be shut in—He does not shut us in—He does not need to—simply take His hand off partly—there is enough disobedience to His law of our bodies all the time to shut us aside—no trouble on that side of the problem—*with pain to Himself,* against His own first will for us, He allows us to be shut in, because only so *can* He get our attention from other things to what He wants done; get us to see things, and think things His way. I am compelled to think it is so.

She said, "I *will* pray." And she was led to pray for her church. Her sister, also a member of the church, lived with her, and was her link with the outer world. Sundays, after church service, the sick woman would ask, "Any special interest in church to-day?" "No," was the constant reply. Wednesday nights, after prayer-meetings, "Any special interest in the service to-night? there must have been." "No; nothing new; same old deacons made the same old prayers."

But one Sunday noon the sister came in from service and asked, "Who do you think preached to-day?" "I don't know, who?" "Why, a stranger from America, a man called Moody, I think was the name." And the sick woman's face turned a bit whiter, and her eye looked half scared, and her lip trembled a bit, and she quietly said: "I know what that means. There's something coming to the old church. Don't bring me any dinner. I must spend this afternoon in prayer." And so she did. And that night in the service that startling change came.

Then to Mr. Moody himself, as he sought her out in her sick room, she told how nearly two years before there came into her hands a copy of a paper published in Chicago called the *Watchman* that contained a talk by Mr. Moody in one of the Chicago meetings, Farwell Hall meetings, I think. All she knew was that talk that made her heart burn, and there was the name M-o-o-d-y. And she was led to pray that God would send that man into their church in London. As simple a prayer as that.

And the months went by, and a year, and over; still she prayed. Nobody knew of it but herself and God. No change seemed to come. Still she prayed. And of course her prayer wrought its purpose. Every Spirit-suggested prayer does. And that is the touchstone of true prayer. And the Spirit of God moved that man of God over to the seaboard, and across the water and into London, and into their church. Then a bit of special siege-prayer, a sort of last charge up the steep hill, and that night the victory came.

Do you not believe—I believe without a doubt, that some day when the night is gone, and the morning light comes up, and we know as we are known, that we shall find that the largest single factor, in that ten days' work, and in the changing of tens of thousands of lives under Moody's leadership is that woman in her praying. Not the only factor, mind you. Moody a man of rare leadership, and consecration, and hundreds of faithful ministers and others rallying to his support. But behind and beneath Moody and the others, and to be reckoned with as first this woman's praying.

Yet I do not know her name. I know Mr. Moody's name. I could name scores of faithful men associated with him in his campaigns, but the name of this one in whom humanly is the secret of it all I do not know. Ah! It is a secret service. We do not know who the great ones are. They tell me she is living yet in the north end of London, and still praying. Shall we pray! Shall we not pray! If something else must slip out, something important, shall we not see to it that intercession has first place!

Making God's Purpose Our Prayer.

With that thought in mind let me this evening suggest a bit of how to pray. As simple a subject as this: how to pray: the how of method.

The first thing in prayer is to find God's purpose, the trend, the swing of it; the second thing to make that purpose our prayer. We want to find out what God is thinking, and then to claim that that shall be done. God is seated up yonder on the throne. Jesus Christ is sitting by His side glorified. Everywhere in the universe God's will is being done except in this corner, called the earth, and its atmosphere, and that bit of the heavens above it where Satan's headquarters are.

It has been done down here by one person—Jesus. He came here to this prodigal planet and did God's will perfectly. He went away. And He has sought and seeks to have men down upon the earth so fully in touch with Himself that He may do in them and through them just what He will. That He may reproduce Himself in these men, and have God's will done again down on the earth. Now prayer is this: finding out God's purpose for our lives, and for the earth and insisting that that shall be done here. The great thing then is to find out and insist upon God's will. And the "how" of method in prayer is concerned with that.

Many a time I have met with a group of persons for prayer. Various special matters for prayer are brought up. Here is this man, needing prayer, and this particular matter, and this one, and this. Then we kneel and pray. And I have many a time thought—not critically in a bad sense—as I have listened to their prayers, as though this is the prayer I must offer:— "Blessed Holy Spirit, Thou knowest this man, and what the lacking thing is in him. There is trouble there. Thou knowest this sick woman, and what the difficulty is there. This problem, and what the hindrance is in it. Blessed Spirit, pray in me the prayer Thou art praying for this man, and this thing, and this one. The prayer Thou art praying, I pray that, in Jesus' name. Thy will be done here under these circumstances."

Sometimes I feel clear as to the particular prayer to offer, but many a time I am puzzled to know. I put this fact with this, but I may not know *all* the facts. I know this man who evidently needs praying for, a Christian man perhaps, his mental characteristics, his conceptions of things, the kind of a will he has, but there may be some fact in there that I do not know, that seriously affects the whole difficulty. And I am compelled to fall back on this: I don't know how to pray as I ought. But the Spirit within me will make intercession for this man as I allow Him to have free swing in me as the medium of His prayer. And He who is listening above as He hears His will for this many being repeated down on the battle-field will recognize His own purpose, of course. And so that thing will be working out because of Jesus' victory over the evil one.

But I may become so sensitive to the Spirit's thoughts and presence, that I shall know more keenly and quickly what to pray for. In so far as I do I become a more skillful partner of His on the earth in getting God's will done.

The Trysting Place.

There are six suggestions here on how to pray. First—we need *time* for prayer, unhurried time, daily time, time enough to forget about how much time it is. I do not mean now: rising in the morning at the very last moment, and dressing, it may be hurriedly, and then kneeling a few moments so as to feel easier in mind: not that. I do not mean the last thing at night when you are jaded and fagged, and almost between the sheets, and then remember and look up a verse and kneel a few moments: not that. That is good so far as it goes. I am not criticising that. Better sweeten and sandwich the day with all of that sort you can get in. But just now I mean this: *taking time* when the mind is fresh and keen, and the spirit sensitive, to thoughtfully pray. We haven't time. Life is so crowded. It must be taken from something else, something important, but still less important than this.

Sacrifice is the continual law of life. The important thing must be sacrificed to the more important. One needs to cultivate a mature judgement, or his strength will be frizzled away in the less important details, and the greater thing go undone, or be done poorly with the fag-ends of strength. If we would become skilled intercessors, and know how to pray simply enough, we must take quiet time daily to get off alone.

The second suggestion: we need a *place* for prayer. Oh! you can pray anywhere, on the street, in the store, travelling, measuring dry goods, hands in dishwater,—where not. But you are not likely to unless you have been off in some quiet place shut in alone with God. The Master said: "Enter into thine inner chamber, and having shut thy door": that door is important. It shuts out, and it shuts in. "Pray to thy Father who is in secret." God is here in this shut-in spot. One must get alone to find out that he never is alone. The more alone we are as far as men are concerned the least alone we are so far as God is concerned.

The quiet place and time are needful to train the ears for keen hearing. A mother will hear the faintest cry of her babe just awaking. It is up-stairs perhaps; the tiniest bit of a sound comes; nobody else hears; but quick as a flash the mother's hands are held quiet, the head alert, then she is off. Her eyes are trained beyond anybody's else; love's training. We need trained ears. A quiet place shuts out the outer sounds, and gives the inner ear a chance to learn other sounds.

A man was standing in a telephone booth trying to talk, but could not make out the message. He kept saying, "I can't hear, I can't hear." The other man by and by said sharply, "If you'll shut that door you can hear." *His* door was shut and he could hear not only the man's voice but the street and store noises too. Some folks have gotten their hearing badly confused because their doors have not been shut enough. Man's voice and God's voice get mixed in their ears. They cannot tell between them. The bother is partly with the door. If you'll shut that door you can hear.

The third suggestion needs much emphasis to-day: *give the Book of God its place in prayer.* Prayer is not talking to God—simply. It is listening first, then talking. Prayer needs three organs of the head, an ear, a tongue and an eye. First an ear to hear what God says, then a tongue to speak, then an eye to look out for the result. Bible study is the listening side of prayer. The purpose of God comes in through the ear, passes through the heart taking on the tinge of your personality, and goes out at the tongue as prayer. It is pathetic what a time God has getting a hearing down here. He is ever speaking but even where there may be some inclination to hear the sounds of earth are choking in our ears the sound of His voice. God speaks in His Word. The most we know of God comes to us here. This Book is God in print. It was inspired, and it *is* inspired. God Himself speaks in this Book. That puts it in a list by itself, quite apart from all others. Studying it keenly, intelligently, reverently will reveal God's great will. What He says will utterly change what you will say.

Our Prayer Teacher.

The fourth suggestion is this: *Let the Spirit teach you how to pray.* The more you pray the more you will find yourself saying to yourself, "I don't know how to pray." Well God understands that. Paul knew that out of his own experience before he wrote it down. And God has a plan to cover our need there. There is One who is a master intercessor. He understands praying perfectly. He is the Spirit of prayer. God has sent Him down to live inside you and me, partly for this, to teach us the fine art of prayer. The suggestion is this: let Him teach you.

When you go alone in the quiet time and place with the Book quietly pray: "blessed Prayer-Spirit, Master-Spirit, teach me how to pray," and He will. Do not be nervous, or agitated, wondering if you will understand. Study to be quiet; mind quiet, body quiet. Be still and listen. Remember Luther's version of David's words.[1] "Be silent to God, and let Him mould thee."

You will find your praying changing. You will talk more simply, like a man transacting business or a child asking, though of course with a reverence and a deepness of feeling not in those things. You will quit asking for some things.

[1]Psalm 37:7.

Some of the old forms of prayer will drop from your lips likely enough. You will use fewer words, maybe, but they will be spoken with a quiet absolute faith that this thing you are asking is being worked out.

This thing of *letting the Spirit teach* must come first in one's praying, and remain to the last, and continue all along as the leading dominant factor. He is a Spirit of prayer peculiarly. The highest law of the Christian life is obedience to the leading of the Holy Spirit. There needs to be a cultivated judgment in reading His leading, and not mistaking our haphazard thoughts as His voice. He should be allowed to teach us how to pray and more, to dominate our praying. The whole range and intensity of the spirit conflict is under His eye. He is God's General on the field of action. There come crises in the battle when the turn of the tide wavers. He knows when a bit of special praying is needed to turn the tide and bring victory. So there needs to be special seasons of persistent prayer, a continuing until victory is assured. Obey His promptings. Sometimes there comes an impulse to pray, or to ask another to pray. And we think, "Why, I have just been praying," *or,* "he does pray about this anyway. It is not necessary to pray again. I do not just like to suggest it." Better obey the impulse quietly, with fewest words of explanation to the other one concerned, or no words beyond simply the request.

Let Him, this wondrous Holy Spirit teach you how to pray. It will take time. You may be a bit set in your way, but if you will just yield and patiently wait, He will teach what to pray, suggest definite things, and often the very language of prayer.

You will notice that the chief purpose of these four suggestions is to learn God's will. The quiet place, the quiet time, the Book, the Spirit—this is the schoolroom as Andrew Murray would finely put it. Here we learn His will. Learning that makes one eager to have it done, and breathes anew the longing prayer that it may be done.

There is a fine word much used in the Psalms, and in Isaiah for this sort of thing—*waiting.* Over and over again that is the word used for that contact with God which reveals to us His will, and imparts to us anew His desires. It is a word full of richest and deepest meaning. Wating is not an occasional nor a hurried thing. It means *steadfastness,* that is holding on; *patience,* that is holding back; *expectancy,* that is holding the face up to see; *obedience,* that is holding one's self in readiness to go or do; it means *listening,* that is holding quiet and still so as to hear.

The Power of a Name.

The fifth suggestion has already been referred to, but should be repeated here. Prayer must be *in Jesus' name.* The relationship of prayer is through Jesus. And the prayer itself must be offered in His name, because the whole strength of the case lies in Jesus. I recall distinctly a certain section of this country where I was for awhile, and very rarely did I hear Jesus' name used in prayer. I heard men, that I knew must be good men, praying in church, in prayer-meeting and elsewhere with no mention of Jesus. Let us distinctly bear in mind that we have no standing with God except through Jesus.

If the keenest lawyer of London, who knew more of American law, and of Illinois statute and of Chicago ordinance—suppose such a case—were to come here, could he plead a case in your court-house? you know he could not. He would have no legal standing here. Now you and I have no standing at yonder bar. We are disbarred through sin. Only as we come through one who has recognized standing there can we come.

But turn that fact around. As we do come in Jesus' name, it is the same as though Jesus prayed. It is the same as though—let me be saying it very softly so it may seem very reverent—as though Jesus put His arm in yours and took you up to the Father, and said, "Father, here is a friend of mine; we're on good terms. Please give him anything he asks, for My sake." And the Father would quickly bend over and graciously say, "What'll you have? You may have anything you ask when My Son asks for it." That is the practical effect of asking in Jesus' name.

But I am very, very clear of this, and I keep swinging back to it, that in the ultimate analysis the force of using Jesus' name is that He is the victor over the traitor prince. Prayer is repeating the Victor's name into the ears of Satan and insisting upon his retreat. As one prays persistently in Jesus' name, the evil one must go. Reluctantly, angrily, he must loosen his clutches, and go back.

The Birthplace of Faith

The sixth suggestion is a familiar one, and yet one much misunderstood. Prayer must be *in faith.* But please note that faith here is not believing that God *can,* but that He *will.* It is kneeling and making the prayer, and then saying, "Father, I thank Thee for this; that it will be so, I thank Thee." Then rising and going about your duties, saying, "that thing is settled." Going again and again, and repeating the prayer with the thanks, and then saying as you go off, "that matter is assured." Not going repeatedly to persuade God. But because prayer is the deciding factor in a spirit conflict and each prayer is like a fresh blow between the eyes of the enemy, a fresh broadside from your fleet upon the fort.

"Well," some one will say, "now you are getting that keyed up rather high. Can we all have faith like that? Can a man *make* himself believe?" There should be no unnatural mechanical insisting that you do believe. Some earnest people make a mistake there. And we will not all have faith like that. That is quite true, and I can easily tell you why. The faith that believes that God *will* do what you ask is not born in a hurry; it is not born in the dust of the street, and the noise of the crowd. But I can tell where that faith will have a birthplace and keep growing stronger: in every heart that takes quiet time off habitually with God, and listens to His voice in His word. Into that heart will come a simple strong faith that the thing it is led to ask shall be accomplished.

That faith has four simple characteristics. It is *intelligent*. It finds out what God's will is. Faith is never contrary to reason. Sometimes it is a bit higher up; the reasoning process has not yet reached up to it. Second, it is *obedient*. It fits its life into God's will. There is apt to be a stiff rub here all the time. Then it is *expectant*. It looks out for the result. It bows down upon the earth, but sends a man to keep an eye on the sea. And then it is *persistent*. It hangs on. It says, "Go again seven times; seventy times seven." It reasons that having learned God's will, and knowing that He does not change, the delay must be caused by the third person, the enemy, and that stubborn persistence in the Victor's name routs him, and leaves a clear field.

A Trained Ear.

In prayer the ear is an organ of first importance. It is of equal importance with the tongue, but must be named first. For the ear leads the way to the tongue. The child hears a word before it speaks it. Through the ear comes the use of the tongue. Where the faculties are normal the tongue is trained only through the ear. This is nature's method. The mind is moulded largely through the ear and eye. It reveals itself, and asserts itself largely through the tongue. What the ear lets in, the mind works over, and the tongue gives out.

This is the order in Isaiah's fiftieth chapter[1] in those words, prophetic of Jesus. "The Lord God hath given me the tongue of them that are taught...He wakeneth my ear to hear as they that are taught." Here the taught tongue came through the awakened ear. One reason why so many of us do not have taught tongues is because we give God so little chance at our ears.

It is a striking fact that the men who have been mightiest in prayer have known God well. They have seemed peculiarly sensitive to Him, and to be overawed with the sense of His love and His greatness. There are three of the Old Testament characters who are particularly mentioned as being mighty in prayer. Jeremiah tells that when God spoke to him about the deep perversity of that nation He exclaimed, "Though Moses and Samuel stood before Me My heart could not be towards this people."[2] When James wants an illustration of a man of prayer for the scattered Jews, he speaks of Elijah, and of one particular crisis in his life, the praying on Carmel's tip-top. These three men are Israel's great men in the great crises of its history. Moses was the maker and moulder of the nation. Samuel was the patient teacher who introduced a new order of things in the national life. Elijah was the rugged leader

[1]Isaiah 50:4.   [2]Jeremiah 15:1.

when the national worship of Jehovah was about to be officially overthrown. These three men, the maker, the teacher, the emergency leader are singled out in the record as peculiarly men of prayer.

Now regarding these men it is most interesting to observe what *listeners* they were to God's voice. Their ears were trained early and trained long, until great acuteness and sensitiveness to God's voice was the result. Special pains seem to have been taken with the first man, the nation's greatest giant, and history's greatest jurist. There were two distinct stages in the training of his ears. First there were the forty years of solitude in the desert sands, alone with the sheep, and the stars, and—God. His ears were being trained by silence. The bustle and confusion of Egypt's busy life were being taken out of his ears. How silent are God's voices. How few men are strong enough to be able to endure silence. For in silence God is speaking to the inner ear.

> "Let us then labour for an inward stillness—
> An inward stillness and an inward healing;
> That perfect silence where the lips and heart
> Are still, and we no longer entertain
> Our own imperfect thoughts and vain opinions,
> But God alone speaks in us, and we wait
> In singleness of heart, that we may know
> His will, and in the silence of our spirits,
> That we may do His will, and do that only."[1]

A gentleman was asked by an artist friend of some note to come to his home, and see a painting just finished. He went at the time appointed, was shown by the attendant into a room which was quite dark, and left there. He was much surprised, but quietly waited developments. After perhaps fifteen min-

[1]Longfellow.

utes his friend came into the room with a cordial greeting, and took him up to the studio to see the painting, which was greatly admired. Before he left the artist said laughingly, "I suppose you thought it queer to be left in that dark room so long." "Yes," the visitor said, "I did." "Well," his friend replied, "I knew that if you came into my studio with the glare of the street in your eyes you could not appreciate the fine colouring of the picture. So I left you in the dark room till the glare had worn out of your eyes."

The first stage of Moses' prayer-training was wearing the noise of Egypt out of his ears so he could hear the quiet fine tones of God's voice. He who would become skilled in prayer must take a silence course in the University of Arabia. Then came the second stage. Forty years were followed by forty days, twice over, of listening to God's speaking voice up in the mount. Such an ear-course as that made a skilled famous intercessor.

Samuel had an earlier course than Moses. While yet a child before his ears had been dulled by earth sounds they were tuned to the hearing of God's voice. The child heart and ear naturally opened upward. They hear easily and believe readily. The roadway of the ear has not been beaten down hard by much travel. God's rains and dews have made it soft, and impressionable. This child's ear was quickly trained to recognize God's voice. And the tented Hebrew nation soon came to know that there was a man in their midst to whom God was talking. O, to keep the heart and inner ear of a child as mature years come!

Of the third of these famous intercessors little is known except of the few striking events in which he figured. Of these, the scene that finds its climax in the opening on Carmel's top of the rain-windows, occupies by far the greater space. And it is notable that the beginning of that long eithteenth chapter of first Kings which tells of the Carmel conflict begins with a message to Elijah from God: "The word of the Lord came to

Elijah:...I will send rain upon the earth." That was the foundation of that persistent praying and sevenfold watching on the mountain-top. First the ear heard, then the voice persistently claimed, and the eye expectantly looked. First the voice of God, then the voice of man. That is the true order. Tremendous results always follow that combination.

Through the Book to God.

With us the training is of the *inner* ear. And its first training, after the early childhood stage is passed, must usually be through the eye. What God has spoken to others has been written down for us. We hear through our eyes. The eye opens the way to the inner ear. God spoke in His word. He is still speaking in it and through it. The whole thought here is to get *to know God*. He reveals Himself in the word that comes from His own lips, and through His messengers' lips. He reveals Himself in His dealings with men. Every incident and experience of these pages is a mirror held up to God's face. In them we may come to see Him.

This is studying the Bible not for the Bible's sake but for the purpose of knowing God. The object aimed at is not the Book but the God revealed in the Book. A man may go to college and take lectures on the English Bible, and increase his knowledge, and enrich his vocabulary, and go away with utterly erroneous ideas of God. He may go to a law school and study the codes of the first great jurist, and get a clear understanding and firm grasp of the Mosaic enactments, as he must do to lay the foundation of legal training, yet he may remain ignorant of God.

He may even go to a Bible school, and be able to analyze and synthesize, give outlines of books, and contents of chapters and much else of that invaluable and indispensable sort of knowledge and yet fail to understand God and His marvellous love-will. It is not the Book with which we are concerned here but the God through the Book. Not to learn truth but through truth to know Him who is Himself the Truth.

There is a fascinating bit of story told of one of David's mighty men.[1] One day there was a sudden attack upon the camp by the Philistines when the fighting men were all away. This man alone was there. The Philistines were the traditional enemy. The very word "Philistines" was one to strike terror to the Hebrew heart. But this man was reckoned one of the first three of David's mighty men because of his conduct that day. He quietly, quickly gripped his sword and fought the enemy single-handed. Up and down, left and right, hip and thigh he smote with such terrific earnestness and drive that the enemy turned and fled. And we are told that the muscles of his hand became so rigid around the handle of his sword that he could not tell by the feeling where his hand stopped, and the sword began. Men and sword were one that day in the action of service against the nation's enemy. When we so absorb this Book, and the Spirit of Him who is its life that people cannot tell the line of division between the man, and the God within the man, then shall we have mightiest power as God's intercessors in defeating the foe. God and man will be as one in the action of service against the enemy.

A Spirit Illumined Mind.

I want to make some simple suggestions for studying this Book so as to get to God through it. There will be the emphasis of doubling back on one's tracks here. For some of the things that should be said have already been said with a different setting. First there must be the *time* element. One must get at least a half hour daily when the mind is fresh. A tired mind does not readily *absorb*. This should be persisted in until there is a habitual spending of at least that much time daily over the Book, with a spirit at leisure from all else, so it can

---

[1] 2 Samuel 23:9, 10.

take in. Then the time should be given to *the Book itself*. If other books are consulted and read as they will be let that be *after* the reading of this Book. Let God talk to you direct, rather than through somebody else. Give Him first chance at your ears. This Book in the central place of your table, the others grouped about it. First time given to it.

A third suggestion brings out the circle of this work. *Read prayerfully.* We learn how to pray by reading prayerfully. This Book does not reveal its sweets and strength to the keen mind merely, but to the spirit enlightened mind. All the mental keenness possible, *with the bright light of the Spirit's illumination*—that is the open sesame. I have sometimes sought the meaning of some passage from a keen scholar who could explain the orientalisms, the fine philological distinctions, the most accurate translations, and all of that, who yet did not seem to know the simple spiritual meaning of the words being discussed. And I have asked the same question of some old saint of God, who did not know Hebrew from a hen's tracks, but who seemed to sense at once the deep spiritual truth taught. The more knowledge, the keener the mind, the better *if* illuminated by the Spirit that inspired these writings.

There is a fourth word to put in here. We must read *thoughtfully.* Thoughtfulness is in danger of being a lost art. Newspapers are so numerous, and literature so abundant, that we are becoming a bright, but a *not thoughtful* people. Often the stream is very wide but has no depth. Fight shallowness. Insist on reading thoughtfully. A very suggestive word in the Bible for this is *"meditate."* Run through and pick out this word with its variations. The word underneath that English word means to mutter, as though a man were repeating something over and over again, as he turned it over in his mind. We have another word, with the same meaning, not much used now—ruminate. We call the cow a ruminant because she chews the cud. She will spend hours chewing the cud, and then give us the rich milk and cream and butter which she has extracted from her food. That is the word here—ruminate. Chew the cud, if you would get the richest cream and butter here.

And it is remarkable how much chewing this Book of God will stand, in comparison with other books. You chew a while on Tennyson, or Browning, or Longfellow. And I am not belittling these noble writings. I have my own favourite among these men. But they do not yield the richest and yet richer cream found here. This Book of God has stood more of that sort of thing than any other, yet it is the freshest book to be found to-day. You read a passage over the two hundredth time and some new fine bit of meaning comes that you had not suspected to be there.

There is a fith suggestion, that is easier to make than to follow. *Read obediently.* As the truth appeals to your conscience *let it change your habit and life.*

> "Light obeyed, increased light:
> Light resisted, bringeth night.
> Who shall give us power to choose
> If the love of light we lose?"[1]

Jesus gives the law of knowledge in His famous words, "If any man willeth to do His will he shall know of the teaching."[2] If we do what we know to do, we will know more. If we know to do, and hesitate and hold back, and do not obey, the inner eye will surely go blind, and the sense of right be dulled and lost. Obedience to truth is the eye of the mind.

Wide Reading

Then one needs to have a *plan* of reading. A consecutive

plan gathers up the fragments of time into a strong whole. Get a good plan, and stick to it. Better a fairly good plan faithfully followed, than the best plan if used brokenly or only occasionally. Probably all the numerous methods of study may be grouped under three general heads, wide reading, topical study, and textual. We all do some textual study in a more or less small way. Digging into a sentence or verse to get at its true and deep meaning. We all do some topical study probably. Gathering up statements on some one subject, studying a character. The more pretentious name is Biblical Theology, finding and arranging all that is taught in the whole range of the Bible on any one theme.

But I want especially to urge *wide reading,* as being the basis of all study. It is the simple, the natural, the scientific method. It is adapted to all classes of persons. I used to suppose it was suited best to college students, and such; but I was mistaken. It is *the* method of all for all. It underlies all methods of getting a grasp of this wonderful Book, and so coming to as full and rounded an understanding of God as is possible to men down here.

By wide reading is meant a *rapid reading through* regardless of verse, chapter, or book divisions. Reading it as *a narrative,* a story. As you would read any book, "The Siege of Pekin," "The Story of an Untold love," to find out the story told, and be able to tell to another. There will be a reverence of spirit with this book that no other inspires, but with the same intellectual method of running through to see what is here. No book is so fascinating as the Bible when read this way. The revised version is greatly to be preferred here simply because it is a *paragraph* version. It is printed more like other books. Some day its printed form will be yet more modernized, and so made easier to read.

To illustrate, begin at the first of Genesis, and read rapidly through *by the page.* Do not try to understand all. You will not. Never mind that now. Just push on. Do not try to remember all. Do not think about that. Let stick to you what will. You will be surprised to find how much will. You may read ten or twelve pages in your first half hour. Next time start in where you left off. You may get through Genesis in three or four times, or less or more, depending on your mood, and how fast your habit of reading may be. You will find a whole Bible in Genesis. A wonderfully fascinating book this Genesis. For love stories, plotting, swift action, beautiful language it more than matches the popular novel.

But do not stop at the close of Genesis. Push on into Exodus. The connection is immediate. It is the same book. And so on into Leviticus. Now do not try to understand Leviticus the first time. You will not the hundredth time perhaps. But you can easily group its contents: these chapters tell of the offerings: these of the law of offerings: here is an incident put in: here sanitary regulations: get the drift of the book. And in it all be getting the picture of God—*that is the one point*. And so on through.

A second stage of this wide reading is fitting together the parts. You know the arrangement of our Bible is not chronological wholly, but topical. The Western mind is almost a slave to chronological order. But the Oriental was not so disturbed. For example, open your Bible to the close of Esther, and again at the close of Malachi. This from Genesis to Esther we all know is the historical section: and this second section the poetical and prophetical section. There is some history in the prophecy, and some prophecy and poetry in the historical part. But in the main this first is historical, and this second poetry and prophecy. These two parts belong together. This first section was not written, and then this second. The second belongs in between the leaves of the first. It was taken out and put by itself because the arrangement of the whole Book is topical rather than chronological.

Now the second stage of wide reading is this: fit these parts

together. Fit the poetry and the prophecy into the history. Do
it on your own account, as though it had never been done. It
has been done much better than you will do it. And you will
make some mistakes. You can check those up afterwards by
some of the scholarly books. And you cannot tell where some
parts belong. But meanwhile the thing to note is this: you are
absorbing the Book. It is becoming a part of you, bone of
your bone, and flesh of your flesh, mentally, and spiritually.
You are drinking in its spirit in huge draughts. There is coming a new vision of God, which will transform radically the
reverent student. In it all seek to acquire *the historical sense.*
That is, put yourself back and see what this thing, or this,
meant to these men, as it was first spoken, under these immediate circumstances.

And so push on into the New Testament. Do not try so
much to fit the four gospels into one connected story,
dovetailing all the parts; but try rather to get a clear grasp of
Jesus' movements those few years as told by these four men.
Fit Paul's letters into the book of Acts, the best you can. The
best book to help in checking up here is Conybeare and
Howson's "Life and Letters of St. Paul." That may well be
one of the books in your collection.

You see at once that this is a method not for a month, nor
for a year, but for years. The topical and textual study grow
naturally out of it. And meanwhile you are getting an intelligent grasp of this wondrous classic, you are absorbing the
finest literature in the English tongue, and infinitely better
yet, you are breathing into your very being a new, deep,
broad, tender conception of *God.*

A Mirror Held up to God's Face.

It is simply fascinating too, to find what light floods these
pages as they are read back in their historical setting, so far as
that is possible. For example turn to the third Psalm, fifth
verse,

"I laid me down and slept;
I awaked; for the Lord sustaineth me."

I was brought up in an old-fashioned church where that was sung. I knew it by heart. As a boy I supposed it meant that night-time had come, and David was sleepy; he had his devotions, and went to bed, and had a good night's sleep. That was all it had suggested to me.

But on my first swing through of the wide reading, my eye was caught, as doubtless yours has often been, by the inscription at the beginning of the psalm: "A psalm of David, *when he fled from Absalom his son.*" Quickly I turned back to Second Samuel to find that story. And I got this picture. David, an old white-haired man, hurrying one day, barefooted, out of his palace, and his capital city, with a few faithful friends, fleeing for his life, because Absalom his favourite son was coming with the strength of the national army to take the kingdom, and his own father's life. And that night as the king lay down to try to catch some sleep, it was upon the bare earth, with only heaven's blue dome for a roof. And as he lay he could almost hear the steady tramp, tramp of the army, over the hills, seeking his throne and his life. Let me ask you, honestly now; do you think you would have slept much that night? I fear I would have been tempted sorely to lie awake thinking: "here I am, an old man, driven from my kingdom, and my home, by my own boy, that I have loved better than my own life." Do you think *you* would have slept much? Tell me.

But David speaking of that night afterwards wrote this down:—"I laid me down, and *slept; I awaked;* (the thought is, I awaked *refreshed*) for the Lord sustaineth me." And I thought, as first that came to me, "I never will have insomnia again: I'll trust." And so you see a lesson of trust in God came, in my wide reading, out of the historical setting, that greatly refreshed and strengthened, and that I have never forgotten. What a God, to give sleep under such circumstances!

A fine illustration of this same thing is found in the New Testament in Paul's letter to the Philippians. At one end of that epistle is this scene: Paul, lying in the inner damp cell of a prison, its small creeping denizens familiarly examining this newcomer, in the darkness of midnight, his back bleeding from the stripes, his bones aching, and his feet fast in the stocks. That is one half of the historical setting of this book. And here is the other half: Paul, a prisoner in Rome. If he tries to ease his body by changing his position, swinging one limb over the other, a chain dangling at his ankle reminds him of the soldier by his side. As he picks up a quill to put a last loving word out of his tender heart for these old friends, a chain pulls at his wrist. That is Philippians, the prison epistle, resounding with clanking chain.

What is the keyword of the book, occurring oftener than any other? Patience? Surely that would be appropriate. Long-suffering? Still more fitting would that seem. But, no, the keyword stands in sharpest contrast to these surroundings. Paul used clouds to make the sun's shining more beautiful. Joy, rejoice, rejoicing, is the music singing all the way through these four chapters. What a wondrous Master, this Jesus, so to inspire His friend doing His will!

Every incident and occurrence of these pages becomes a mirror held up to God's face that we may see how wondrous He is.

> "Upon Thy Word I rest
>   Each pilgrim day.
> This golden staff is best
>   For all the way.
> What Jesus Christ hath spoken,
>   Cannot be broken!

"Upon Thy Word I rest;
  So strong, so sure,
So full of comfort blest,
  So sweet, so pure:
The charter of salvation:
  Faith's broad foundation.

"Upon They Word I stand:
  That cannot lie.
Christ seals it in my hand.
  He cannot lie.
Thy Word that faileth never:
  Abiding ever."[1]

[1]Frances Ridley Havergal.

He Came to His Own

The purpose of prayer is to get God's will done. What a stranger God is in His own world! Nobody is so much slandered as He. He comes to His own, and they keep Him standing outside the door, like a pilgrim of the night, staff in hand, while they peer suspiciously at Him through the crack of the hinges.

Some of us shrink back from making a full surrender of life to God. And if the real reason were known it would be found to be that we are *afraid* of God. We fear He will put something bitter in the cup, or some rough thing in the road. And without doubt the reason we are afraid of God is because we do not *know* God. The great prayer of Jesus' heart that night with the eleven was, "that they may *know* Thee the only true God, and Jesus Christ whom Thou didst send."

To understand God's will we must understand something of His character, Himself. There are five common every-day words I want to bring you to suggest something of who God is. They are familiar words, in constant use. The first is the word *father*. "Father" stands for strength, loving strength. A father plans, and provides for, and protects his loved ones. All fathers are not good. How man can extract the meaning out of a fine word, and use the word without its meaning. If you will think of the finest father ever you knew that anybody ever had; think of him now. Then remember this, God is a father, only He is so much finer a father than the finest father you ever knew of. And His will for your *life*—I am not talking about heaven, and our souls just now, that is in it too—His will for your life down here these days is a father's will for the one most dearly loved.

The second word is a finer word. Because woman is finer than man, and was made, and meant to be, this second word is finer than the first. I mean the word *mother*. If father stands for strength, mother stands for love,—great, patient, tender, fine-fibred, enduring love. What would she not do for her loved one! Why, not unlikely she went down into the valley of the shadow that that life might come; and did it gladly with the love-light shining out of her eyes. Yes, and would do it again, that the life may remain if need be. That is a mother. You think of the finest mother ever you knew. And the suggestion brings the most hallowed memories to my own heart. Then remember this: God is a mother, only He is so much finer a mother than the finest mother you ever knew.

The references in scripture to God as a mother are numerous. "Under His wings" is a mother figure. The mother-bird gathers her brood up under her wings to feel the heat of her body, and for protection. The word mother is not used for God in the Bible. I think it is because with God "father" includes "mother." It takes more of the human to tell the story than of the divine. With God, all the strength of the father and all the fine love of the mother are combined in that word "father." And His will for us is a mother's will, a wise loving mother's will for the darling of her heart.

The third word is *friend*. I do not mean to use it in the cheaper meaning. There is a certain kindliness of speech in which all acquaintances are called friends. Tupper says, we call all men friends who are not known to be enemies. But I mean to use the word in its finer meaning. Her, a friend is one who loves you for your sake only and steadfastly loves without regard to any return, even a return-love. The English have a saying that you may fill a church with your acquaintances, and not fill the pulpit seats with your friends. If you may have in your life one or two real friends you are very wealthy. If you will think for a moment of the very best friend you ever knew anybody to have. Then remember this: God is a friend. Only He is ever so much better a friend than the best friend you ever knew of. And the plan He has thought out for your life is such a one as that word would suggest.

The fourth word, I almost hesitate to use, yet I am sure I need not here. The hesitancy is because the word and its relationship are spoken of lightly, frivolously, so much, even in good circles. I mean that rare fine word *lover*. Where two have met, and acquaintance has deepened into friendship, and that in turn into the holiest emotion, the highest friendship. What would he not do for her! She becomes the new human centre of his life. In a good sense he worships the ground she treads upon. And she—she will leave wealth for poverty if only so she may be with him in the coming days. She will leave home and friends, and go to the ends of the earth if his service calls him there. You think of the finest lover, man or woman, you ever knew anybody to have. Then remember this, let me say it in soft, reverent tones, God is a lover—shall I say in yet more reverent voice, a sweet-heart-lover. Only He is so much finer a lover than the finest lover you ever knew of. And His will, His plan for your life and mine—it hushes my heart to say it—is a lover's plan for his loved one.

The fifth word is this fourth word a degree finer spun, a stage farther on, and higher up, the word *husband*. This is the word on the man side for the most hallowed relationship of earth. This is the lover relationship in its perfection stage. With men husband is not always a finer word than lover. The more's the pity. How man does cheapen God's plan of things; leaves out the kernel, and keeps only an empty shell sometimes. In God's thought a husband is a lover *plus*. He is all that the finest lover is, and more; more tender, more eager, more thoughtful. Two lives are joined, and begin living one life. Two wills, yet one. Two persons, yet one purpose. Duality in unity. Will you call to mind for a moment the best husband you ever knew any woman to have. Then remember this that God is a husband; only He is an infinitely more thoughtful husband than any you ever knew. And His will for your life is a husband's will for his life's friend and companion.

Now, please, do not *you* take one of these words, and say, "I like that"; and *you* another and say, "That conception of God sppeals to me," and *you* another. How we do whittle God down to our narrow conceptions! You must take all five words, and think the finest meaning into each, and then put them all together, to get a close up idea of God. He is all that, *and more*.

You see God is so much that it takes a number of earth's relationships put together to get a good suggestion of what He is. He is a father, a mother, a friend, a lover, a husband. I have not brought book, and chapter, and verse. But you know I could spend a long time with you reading over the numerous passages giving these conceptions of God.

And God's will for us is the plan of such a God as that. It includes the body, health and strength; the family and home matters; money and business matters; friendships, including the choice of life's chief friend; it includes service, what service and where; and constant guidance; it includes the whole life, and the world of lives. All this He has thought into, lovingly, carefully. Does a wise mother think of her child's needs into the details, the necessities and the love extras? That is God.

The One Purpose of Prayer.

Now, the whole thought in prayer is to get the will of a God like that done in our lives and upon this old earth. The greatest prayer any one can offer is, "Thy will be done." It will be offered in a thousand different forms, with a thousand details, as needs arise daily. But every true prayer comes under those four words. There is not a good desirable thing that you have thought of that He has not thought of first, and probably with an added touch not in your thought. Not to grit your teeth and lock your jaw and pray for grace to say, "Thy will be *endured:* it is bitter, but I must be resigned; that is a Christian grace; Thy will be *endured.*" Not that, please. Do not slander God like that. There is a superficial idea among men that charges God with many misfortunes and ills for which He is not at all responsible. He is continually doing the very best that can be done under the circumstances for the best results. He has a bad mixture of stubborn warped human wills to deal with. With infinite patience and skill and diplomacy and success too He is ever working at the tangled skein of human life, through the human will.

It may help us here to remember that God has a first and a second will for us: a first choice and a second. He always prefers that His first will shall be accomplished in us. But where we will not be wooed up to that height, He comes down to the highest level we will come up to, and works with us there. For instance, God's first choice for Israel was that He Himself should be their king. There was to be no human, visible king, as with the surrounding nations. He was to be their king. They were to be peculiar in this. But to Samuel's sorrow and yet more to God's, they insisted upon a king. And so God gave them a king. And David the great shepherd-psalmist-king was a man after God's own heart, and the world's Saviour came of the Davidic line. God did His best upon the level they chose and a great best it was. Yet the human king and line of kings was not God's first will, but a second will yielded to because the first would not be accepted. God is ever doing the best for human lives than can be done through the human will.

His first will for our bodies, without doubt, is that there should be a strong healthy body for each of us. But there is a far higher thing being aimed at in us than that. And with keen pain to His own heart, He oft times permits bodily weakness and suffering because in the conditions of our wills only so can these higher and highest things be gotten at. And where the human will comes into intelligent touch with Himself, and the higher can so be reached, with great gladness and eagerness the bodily difficulty is removed by Him.

There are two things, at least, that modify God's first will for us. First of all the degree of our intelligent willingness that He shall have His full sway. And second, the circumstances of one's life. Each of us is the centre of a circle of people, an ever changing circle. If we be in touch with Him God is speaking through each of us to his circle. Our experiences with God: His dealings with us, under the varying circumstances are a part of His message to that circle. God is trying to win men. It takes marvellous diplomacy on His part. And God is a wondrous tactitian. But—very reverently—He is a needy God. He needs us to help Him, each in his circle. We must be perfectly willing to have His will done; and more, we must trust Him to know what is best to do in us and with us in the circle of our circumstances. God is a great economist. He wastes no forces. Every bit is being conserved towards the great end in view.

There may be a false submission to His supposed will in some affliction; a not reaching out after *all* that He has for us. And at the other swing of the pendulum there may be a sort of *logical praying* for some desirable thing because a friend tells us we should claim it. By logical praying I mean the studying of a statement of God's word, and possibly some one's explanation of it, and hearing or knowing how somebody else has claimed a certain thing through that statement and then concluding that therefore we should so claim. The trouble with that is that it stops too soon. Praying in the Spirit as opposed to logical praying is doing this logical thinking: *then* quietly taking all to God, to learn what His will is for *you,* under your circumstances, and in the circle of people whom He touches through you.

The Spirit's Prayer Room.

There is a remarkable passage in Paul's Roman letter about prayer and God's will.[1] "And in like manner the Spirit also helpeth our infirmity: for we know not how to pray as we ought; but the Spirit Himself maketh intercession for us with groanings which cannot be uttered; and He that searcheth the hearts knoweth what is the mind of the Spirit, that He maketh intercession for the saints according to the will of God."

Please notice: these words connect back with the verses ending with verse seventeen. Verses eighteen to twenty-five are a parenthesis. As the Spirit within breathes out the "Father" cry of a child, which is the prayer-cry, so He helps us in praying. It is our infirmity that we do not know how to pray *as we ought*. There is willingness and eagerness too. No bother there. But a lack of knowledge. We don't know how. But the Spirit knows how. He is the master-prayer. He knows God's will perfectly. He knows what best to be praying under all circumstances. And He is within you and me. He is there as a prayer-spirit. He prompts us to pray. He calls us away to the quiet room to our knees. He inclines to prayer wherever we are. He is thinking thoughts that find no response in us. They cannot be expressed in our lips for they are not in our thinking. He prays with an intensity quite beyond the possibility of language to express. And the heart-searcher—God listening above—knows fully what this praying Spirit is thinking within me, and wordlessly praying, for they are one. He recognizes His own purposes and plans being repeated in this man down on the earth by His own Spirit.

And the great truth is that the Spirit within us prays God's will. He teaches us God's will. He teaches us how to pray God's will. And He Himself prays God's will in us. And further that He seeks to pray God's will—that is to pray for the thing God has planned—in us before we have yet reached up to where we know ourselves what that will is.

We should be ambitious to cultivate a healthy sensitiveness to this indwelling Spirit. And when there comes that quick inner wooing away to pray let us faithfully obey. Even though we be not clear what the particular petition is to be let us remain in prayer while He uses us as the medium of His praying.

Oftentimes the best prayer to offer about some friend, or some particular thing, after perhaps stating the case the best we can is this: "Holy Spirit, be praying in me the thing the Father wants done. Father, what the Spirit within me is praying, that is my prayer in Jesus' name. They will, what Thou art wishing and thinking, may that be fully done here."

How to Find God's Will.

We should make a study of God's will. We ought to seek to become skilled in knowing His will. The more we know Him the better shall we be able to read intelligently His will.

It may be said that God has two wills for each of us, or, better, there are two parts to His will. There is His will of grace, and His will of government. His will of grace is plainly revealed in His Word. It is that we shall be saved, and made holy, and pure, and by and by glorified in His own presence. His will of government is His particular plan for my life. God has ever life planned. The highest possible ambition for a life is to reach God's plan. He reveals that to us bit by bit as we need to know. If the life is to be one of special service He will make that plain, what service, and where, and when. Then each next step He will make plain.

Learning His will here hinges upon three things, simple enough but essential. I must keep *in touch* with Him so He has an open ear to talk into. I must *delight* to do His will, *because it is His.* The third thing needs special emphasis. Many who are right on the first two stumble here, and sometimes measure their length on the ground. *His Word must be allowed to discipline my judgment as to Himself and His will.* Many of us stumble on number one and on number two. And very many willing earnest men sprawl badly when it comes to number three. The bother with these is the lack of disciplined judgment about God and His will. If we would prayerfully *absorb* the Book, there would come a better poised judgment. We need to get a broad sweep of God's thought, to breathe Him in as He reveals Himself in this Book. The meek man—that is the man willing to yield his will to a higher will—will He guide in his judgement, that is, in his mental processes.[1]

This is John's standpoint in that famous passage in his first epistle.[2] "And this is the boldness that we have towards Him, that, if we ask anything according to His will, He heareth us: and if we know that He heareth us whatsoever we ask, we know that we have the petitions that we have asked of Him." These words dovetail with great nicety into those already quoted from Paul in the eighth of Romans. The whole supposition here is that we have learned His will about the particular matter in hand. Having gotten that footing, we go to prayer with great boldness. For if He wants a thing and I want it and we join—that combination cannot be broken.

God's Door into a Home.

The heart of God hungers to redeem the world. For that
He gave His own, only Son, though the treatment He received
tore that Father's heart to the bleeding. For that He sent the
Holy Spirit to do in men what the Son had done for them.
For that He placed in human hands the mightiest of all
forces—prayer, that so we might become partners with Him.

For that too He set man in the relationships of kinship and
friendship. He wins men through men. Man is the goal, and
he is also the road to the goal. Man is the object aimed at.
And he is the medium of approach, whether the advance be
by God or by Satan. God will not enter a man's heart without
his consent, and Satan *can*not. God would reach men
through men, and Satan must. And so God has set us in the
strongest relation that binds men, the relation of love, that
He may touch one through another. Kinship is a relation
peculiar to man, and to the earth.

I have at times been asked by some earnest sensitive persons if it is not selfish to be especially concerned for one's
own, over whom the heart yearns much, and the prayer offered is more tender and intense and more frequent. Well, if
you do not pray for them who will? Who *can* pray for them
with such believing persistent fervour as you! God has set us
in the relationship of personal affection and of kinship for
just such a purpose. He binds us together with the ties of love
that we may be concerned for each other. If there be but one
in a home in touch with God, that one becomes God's door
into the whole family.

Contact means opportunity, and that in turn means
responsibility. The closer the contact the greater the opportunity and the greater too the responsibility. Unselfishness
does not mean to exclude one's self, and one's own. It means
right proportions in our perspective. Humility is not whip-

ping one's self. It is forgetting one's self in the thought of others. Yet even that may be carried to a bad extreme. Not only is it not selfish so to pray, it is a part of God's plan that we should so pray. I am most responsible for the one to whom I am most closely related.

A Free Agent Enslaved.

One of the questions that is more often asked in this connection than any other perhaps is this: may we pray with assurance for the conversion of our loved ones? No question sets more hearts in an audience to beating faster than does that. I remember speaking in the Boston noonday meeting, in the old Broomfield Street M. E. Church on this subject one week. Perhaps I was speaking rather positively. And at the close of the meeting one day a keen, cultured Christian woman whom I knew came up for a word. She said, "I do not think we can pray like that." And I said, "Why not?" She paused a moment, and her well-controlled agitation revealed in eye and lip told me how deeply her thoughts were stirred. Then she said quietly, "I have a brother. He is not a Christian. The theatre, the win, the club, the cards—that is his life. And he laughs at me. I would rather than anything else that my brother were a Christian. But," she said, and here both her keenness and the training of her early teaching came in, "I do not think I can pray positively for his conversion, for he is a free agent, is he not? And God will not save a man against his will."

I want to say to you to-day what I said to her. Man *is* a free agent, to use the old phrase, so far as God is concerned; utterly, wholly free. *And,* he is the most enslaved agent on the earth, so far as sin, and selfishness and prejudice are concerned. The purpose of our praying is not to force or coerce his will; never that. It is to *free* his will of the warping influences that now twist it awry. It is to get the dust out of his eyes so his sight shall be clear. And once he is free, able to see aright, to balance things without prejudice, the whole probability is in favour of his using his will to choose the only right.

I want to suggest to you the ideal prayer for such a one. It is an adaptation of Jesus' own words. It may be pleaded with much variety of detail. It is this: deliver him from the evil one; and work in him *Thy will* for him, by Thy power to Thy glory in Jesus, the Victor's name. And there are three special passages upon which to base this prayer. First Timothy, second chapter, fourth verse (American version), "God our Saviour, who would have all men to be saved." That is God's will for your loved one. Second Peter, third chapter, ninth verse, "not wishing (or willing) that any should perish but that all should come to repentance." That is God's will, or desire, for the one you are thinking of now. The third passage is on our side who do the praying. It tells who may offer this prayer with assurance. John, fifteenth chapter, seventh verse, "If ye abide in Me, and My words abide in you, you ask what it is your will to ask, and I will bring it to pass for you."

There is a statement of Paul's in second Timothy that graphically pictures this:[1] "The Lord's servant must not strive"—not argue, nor combat—"but be gentle towards all, apt to teach"—ready and skilled in explaining, helping—"in meakness correcting (or, instructing) them that oppose themselves; if peradventure God may give them repentance unto the knowledge of the truth, and *thy may recover themselves out of the snare of the devil,* having been taken captive by him unto his will."

That word "deliver" in this prayer, as used by Jesus, the word under our English, has a picturesque meaning. It means *rescue.* Here is a man taken captive, and in chains. But he has become infatuated with his captor, and is befooled regarding his condition. Our prayer is, "rescue him from the evil one," and because Jesus is Victor over the captor, the rescue will take place.

Without any doubt we may assure the conversion of these

laid upon our hearts by such praying. The prayer in Jesus' name drives the enemy off the battle-field of the man's will, and leaves him free to choose aright. There is one exception to be noted, a very, very rare exception. There may be *extreme* instances where such a prayer may not be offered; where the spirit of prayer is withdrawn. But such are very rare and extreme, and the conviction regarding that will be unmistakable beyond asking any questions.

And I cannot resist the conviction—I greatly dislike to say this, I would much rather not if I regarded either my own feelings or yours. But I cannot resist the conviction—listen very quietly, so I may speak in quietest tones—that there are people...in that lower, lost world...who are there... because some one failed to put his life in touch with God, and pray.

The Place Where God is Not.

Having said that much let me go on to say this further, and please let me say it all in softest sobbing voice—there is a hell. There must be a hell. You may leave this Bible sheer out of your reckoning in the matter. Still there must be a place for which that word of ugliest associations is the word to use. *Philosophically* there must be a hell. That is the name for the place where God is not; for the place where they will gather together who insist on leaving God out. God out! There can be no worse hell than that! God away! Man held back by no restraints!

I am very clear it is *not* what men have pictured it to be. It is not what my childish fancy saw and shrank from terrified. And, please let us be very careful that we never consign anybody there, in our thinking or speaking about them. When that life whose future might be questioned has gone the most we can say is that we leave it with a God infinitely just and the personification of love.

There has been in some quarters an unthinking consigning

of persons to a lost world. And there has been in our day a clean swing of the pendulum to the other extreme. Both drifts are to be dreaded. Let us deal very tenderly here, yet with a right plainness in our tenderness. We are to warn men faithfully. We know the Book's plain teaching that these who prefer to leave God out "shall go away." The going is of their own accord and choice. Regarding particular ones we do not know and are best silent. The grave is closing. Let us deal with the living.

One day at the close of the morning hour at a Bible conference in the Alleghany Mountains a young woman came up for a moment's conversation. She spoke about a friend, not a professing Christian, for whom she had prayed much, and who had died unexpectedly. He had passed away during unconsciousness, with no opportunity for exchange of words. She was much agitated as the facts were recited, and then said as she finished, "he is lost and in hell: and I can never pray again."

We talked quietly awhile and I gathered the following facts. He was of a Christian family, perfectly familiar with the Bible, was a thoughtful man, of outwardly correct life in the main, had talked about these matters with others but had never either in conversation or more openly confessed personal faith in Christ. He was not in good health. Then came the sudden end. One other fact came out. She had prayed for his conversion for a long time. She was herself an earnest Christian woman, solicitous for others. There were four facts to go upon regarding him. He knew the way to God. He was thoughtful. He had never openly accepted. Some one had prayed.

Can one *know* anything certainly about that man's condition? There are two sorts of knowledge, direct and inferential. I know there is such a city as London for I have walked its streets. That is direct knowledge. I know there is such a city as St. Petersburg because though I have never been there, yet through my reading, pictures I have seen, and friends who have been there I am clear of its existence to the point of *knowledge*. That is inferential knowledge.

Now regarding this man after he slipped from the grasp of his friends, I have no direct knowledge. But I have very positive inferential knowledge based upon these four facts. Three of the facts, namely, the first, second, and fourth were favourable to the end desired. The third swings neither way. The great dominant fact in the case is the fourth, and a great and dominating fact it is in judging—some one in touch with God had been persistently, believingly praying up to the time of the quick end. That fact with the others gives strong inferential knowledge regarding the man. It is sufficient to comfort a heart, and give one renewed faith in praying for others.

Saving the Life.

We cannot know a man's mental processes. This is surely true, that if in the very last half-twinkling of an eye a man look up towards God longingly, that look is the turning of the will to God. And that is quite enough. God is eagerly watching with hungry eyes for the quick turn of a human eye up to Himself. Doubtless many a man has so turned in the last moment of his life when we were not conscious of his consciousness, nor aware of the movements of his outwardly unconsciousness subconsciousness. One may be unconscious of outer things, and yet be keenly conscious towards God.

At another of these summer gatherings this incident came to me. A man seemingly of mature mind and judgment told me of a friend of his. That was as close as I got to the friend himself. This friend was not a professing Christian, was thrown from a boat, sank twice and perhaps three times, and then was rescued, and after some difficulty resuscitated. He told afterwards how swiftly his thoughts came as they are said to do to one in such circumstances. He thought surely he was drowning, was quiet in his mind, thought of God and how he had not been trusting Him, and in his thought he prayed for forgiveness. He lived afterwards a consistent Christian life. This illustrates simply the possibilities open to one in his keen inner mental processes.

Here is surely enough knowledge to comfort many a bereft heart, and enough too to make us pray persistently and believingly for loved ones because of prayer's uncalculated and incalculable power. Be sure the prayer-fact is in the case of *your* friend, *and is strong*.

Yet let us be wary, very wary of letting this influence us one bit farther. That man is nothing less than a fool who presumes upon such statements to resist God's gracious pleadings for his life. And on our side, we must not fail to warn men lovingly, tenderly yet with plainness of the tremendous danger of delay, in coming to God. A man may be so stupefied at the close as to shut out of his range what has been suggested here. And further even if a man's soul be saved he is responsible to God for his life. We want men to *live* for Jesus, and win others to Him. And further, yet, reward, preferment, honour in God's kingdom depends upon faithfulness to Him down here. Who would be saved by the skin of his teeth!

The great fact to have burned in deep is that we may assure the coming to God of our loved ones with their lives, as well as for their souls if we will but press the battle.

Giving God a Clear Road for Action.

Out in one of the trans-Mississippi states I ran across an illustration of prayer in real life that caught me at once, and has greatly helped me in understanding prayer.

Fact is more fascinating than fiction. If one could know what is going on around him, how surprised and startled he would be. If we could get *all* the facts in any one incident, and get them colourlessly, and have the judgment to sift and analyze accurately, what fascinating instances of the power of prayer would be disclosed.

There is a double side to this story. The side of the man who was changed, and the side of the woman who prayed. He is a New Englander, by birth and breeding, now living in this western state: almost a giant physically, keen mentally, a lawyer, and a natural leader. He had the conviction as a boy that if he became a Christian he was to preach. But he grew up a skeptic, read up and lectured on skeptical subjects. He was the representative of a district of his western home state in congress; in his fourth term or so I think at this time.

The experience I am telling came during that congress when the Hayes-Tilden controversy was up, the intensest congress Washington has known since the Civil War. It was not a time specially suited to meditation about God in the halls of congress. And further he said to me that somehow he knew all the other skeptics who were in the lower house and they drifted together a good bit and strengthened each other by their talk.

One day as he was in his seat in the lower house, in the midst of the business of the hour, there came to him a conviction that God—the God in whom he did not believe, whose existence he could keenly disprove—God was right there above his head thinking about him, and displeased at the way he was behaving towards Him. And he said to himself: "this is ridiculous, absurd. I've been working too hard; confined too closely; my mind is getting morbid. I'll go out, and get some fresh air, and shake myself." And so he did. But the conviction only deepened and intensified. Day by day it grew. And that went on for weeks, into the fourth month as I recall his words. Then he planned to return home to attend to some business matters, and to attend to some preliminaries for securing the nomination for the governorship of his state. And as I understand he was in a fair way to securing the nomination, so far as one can judge of such matters. And his party is the dominant party in the state. A nomination for governor by his party has usually been followed by election.

He reached his home and had hardly gotten there before he found that his wife and two others had entered into a holy compact of prayer for his conversion, and had been so praying for some months. Instantly he thought of his peculiar unwelcome Washington experience, and became intensely interested. But not wishing them to know of his interest, he asked carelessly when "this thing began." His wife told him the day. He did some quick mental figuring, and he said to me, "I knew almost instantly that the day she named fitted into the calendar with the coming of that conviction or impression about God's presence."

He was greatly startled. He wanted to be thoroughly honest in all his thinking. And he said he knew that if a single fact of that sort could be established, of prayer producing such results, it carried the whole Christian scheme of belief with it. And he did some stiff fighting within. He had been wrong all those years? He sifted the matter back and forth as a lawyer would the evidence in any case. And he said to me, "As an honest man I was compelled to admit the facts, and I believe I might have been led to Christ that very night."

A few nights later he knelt at the altar in the Methodist meeting-house in his home town and surrendered his strong will to God. Then the early conviction of his boyhood days came back. He was to preach the gospel. And like Saul of old, he utterly changed his life, and has been preaching the gospel with power ever since.

Then I was intensely fascinated in getting the other side, the praying-side of the story. His wife had been a Christian for years, since before their marriage. But in some meetings in the home church she was led into a new, a full surrender to Jesus Christ as Master, and had experienced a new consciousness of the Holy Spirit's presence and power. Almost at once came a new intense desire for her husband's conversion.

The compact of three was agreed upon, of daily prayer for him until the change came.

As she prayed that night after retiring to her sleeping apartment she was in great distress of mind in thinking and praying for him. She could get no rest from this intense distress. At length she rose, and knelt by the bedside to pray. As she was praying and distressed a voice, an exquisitely quiet inner voice said, "will you abide the consequences?" She was startled. Such a thing was wholly new to her. She did not know what it meant. And without paying any attention to it, went on praying. Again came the same quietly spoken words to her ear, "will you abide the consequences?" And again the half frightened feeling. She slipped back to bed to sleep. But sleep did not come. And back again to her knees, and again the patient, quiet voice.

This time with an earnestness bearing the impress of her agony she said, "Lord, I will abide any consequence that may come if only my husband may be brought to Thee." And at once the distress slipped away, and a new sweet peace filled her being, and sleep quickly came. And while she prayed on for weeks and months patiently, persistently, day by day, the distress was gone, the sweet peace remained in the assurance that the result was surely coming. And so it was coming all those days down in the thick air of Washington's lower house, and so it did come.

What *was* the consequence to her? She was a congressman's wife. She would likely have been, so far as such matters may be judged, the wife of the governor of her state, the first lady socially of the state. She is a Methodist minister's wife changing her home every few years. A very different position in many ways. No woman will be indifferent to the social difference involved. Yet rarely have I met a woman with more of that fine beauty which the peace of God brings, in her glad face, and in her winsome smile.

Do you see the simple philosophy of that experience. Her

surrender gave God a clear channel into that man's will. When the roadway was cleared, her prayer was a spirit-force traversing instantly the hundreds of intervening miles, and affecting the spirit-atmosphere of his presence.

Shall we not put our wills fully in touch with God, and sheer out of sympathy with the other one, and persistently plead and claim for each loved one, "deliver him from the evil one, and work in him Thy will, to Thy glory, by Thy power, in the Victor's name." And then add amen—so it *shall* be. Not so *may* it be—a wish, but so it *shall* be—an expression of confidence in Jesus' power. *And these lives shall be won, and these souls saved.*

IV. JESUS' HABITS OF PRAYER

A Pen Sketch.

When God would win back His prodigal world He sent down a Man. That Man while more than man insisted upon being truly a man. He touched human life at every point. No man seems to have understood prayer, and to have prayed as did He. How can we better conclude these quiet talks on prayer than by gathering about His person and studying His habits of prayer.

A habit is an act repeated so often as to be done involuntarily; that is, without a new decision of the mind each time it is done.

Jesus prayed. He loved to pray. Sometimes praying was His way of resting. He prayed so much and so often that it became a part of His life. It became to Him like breathing—involuntary.

There is no thing we need so much as to learn how to pray. There are two ways of receiving instruction; one, by being told; the other, by watching some one else. The latter is the simpler and the surer way. How better can we learn how to pray than by watching how Jesus prayed, and then trying to imitate Him. Not, just now, studying what He *said* about prayer, invaluable as that is, and so closely interwoven with the other; nor yet how He received the requests of men when on earth, full of inspiring suggestion as that is of His *present* attitude towards our prayers; but how He Himself prayed when down here surrounded by our same circumstances and temptations.

There are two sections of the Bible to which we at once turn for light, the gospels and the Psalms. In the gospels is given chiefly the *outer* side of His prayer-habits; and in certain of the Psalms, glimpses of the *inner* side are unmistakably revealed.

Turning now to the gospels, we find the picture of the praying Jesus like an etching, a sketch in black and white, the fewest possible strokes of the pen, a scratch here, a line there, frequently a single word added by one writer to the narrative of the others, which gradually bring to view the outline of a long figure with upturned face.

Of the fifteen mentions of His praying found in the four gospels, it is interesting to note that while Matthew gives three, and Mark and John each four, it is Luke, Paul's companion and mirror-like friend, who, in eleven such allusions, supplies most of the picture.

Does this not contain a strong hint of the explanation of that other etching plainly traceable in the epistles which reveals Paul's own marvellous prayer-life?

Matthew, immersed in the Hebrew Scriptures, writes to the Jews of their promised Davidic King; Mark, with rapid pen, relates the ceaseless activity of this wonderful servant of the Father. John, with imprisoned body, but rare liberty of vision, from the glory-side revealed on Patmos, depicts the Son of God coming on an errand from the Father into the world, and again, leaving the world and going back home unto the Father. But Luke emphasizes the *human* Jesus, a *Man*—with reverence let me use a word in its old-fashioned meaning—a *fellow,* that is, one of ourselves. And the Holy Spirit makes it very plain throughout Luke's narrative that the *man* Christ Jesus *prayed;* prayed *much; needed* to pray; *loved* to pray.

Oh! when shall we men down here, sent into the world as He was sent into the world, with the same mission, the same field, the same Satan to combat, the same Holy Spirit to empower, find out that power lies in keeping closest connection with the Sender, and completest insulation from the power-absorbing world!

Dissolving Views.

Let me rapidly sketch those fifteen mentions of the gospel writers, attempting to keep their chronological order.

The first mention is by Luke, in chapter three. The first

three gospels all tell of Jesus' double baptism, but it is Luke who adds, "and praying." It was while waiting in prayer that He received the gift of the Holy Spirit. He *dared* not begin His public mission without that anointing. It had been promised in the prophetic writings. And now, standing in the Jordan, He waits and prays until the blue above is burst through by the gleams of glory-light from the upper-side and the dove-like Spirit wings down and abides upon Him. *Prayer brings power.* Prayer *is* power. The time of prayer is the time of power. The place of prayer is the place of power. Prayer is tightening the connections with the divine dynamo so that the power may flow freely without loss or interruption.

The second mention is made by Mark in chapter one. Luke, in chapter four, hints at it, "when it was day He came out and went into a desert place." But Mark tells us plainly "in the morning a great while before the day (or a little more literally, 'very early while it was yet very dark') He arose and went out into the desert or solitary place and there prayed." The day before, a Sabbath day spent in His adopted hometown Capernaum, had been a very busy day for Him, teaching in the synagogue service, the interruption by a demon-possessed man, the casting out amid a painful scene; afterwards the healing of Peter's mother-in-law, and then at sun-setting the great crowd of diseased and demonized thronging the narrow street until far into the night, while He, passing amongst them, by person touch, healed and restored every one. It was a long and exhausting day's work. One of us spending as busy a Sabbath would probably feel that the next morning needed an extra hour's sleep if possible. One must rest surely. But this man Jesus seemed to have another way of resting in addition to sleep. Probably He occupied the guest-chamber in Peter's home. The house was likely astir at the usual hour, and by and by breakfast was ready, but the Master had not appeared yet, so they waited a bit. After a while the maid slips to His room door and taps lightly, but there's no answer; again a little bolder knock, then pushing the door ajar she finds the room unoccupied. Where's the Master? "Ah!" Peter says; "I think I know. I have noticed before this that He has a way of slipping off early in the morning to some quiet place where He can be alone." And a little knot of disciples with Peter in the lead starts out on a search for Him, for already a crowd is gathering at the door and filling the street again, hungry for more. And they "tracked Him down" here and there on the hillsides, among clumps of trees, until suddenly they come upon Him quietly praying with a wondrous calm in His great eyes. Listen to Peter as he eagerly blurts out, "Master, there's a big crowd down there, all asking for you." But the Master's quiet decisive tones reply, "Let us go into the next towns that I may preach there also; for to this end came I forth." Much easier to go back and deal again with the old crowd of yesterday; harder to meet the new crowds with their new skepticism, but there's not doubt about what *should* be done. Prayer wonderfully clears the vision; steadies the nerves; defines duty; stiffens the purpose; sweetens and strengthens the spirit. The busier the day for Him the more surely must the morning appointment be kept,[1] and even an earlier start made, apparently. The more virtue went forth from Him, the more certainly must He spend time, and even *more* time, alone with Him who is the source of power.

The third mention is in Luke, chapter five. Not a great while after the scene just described, possibly while on the trip suggested by His answer to Peter, in some one of the numerous Gallilean villages, moved with the compassion that ever burned His heart, He had healed a badly diseased leper, who, disregarding His express command, so widely published the fact of His remarkable healing that great crowds blocked Jesus' way in the village and compelled Him to go out to the

---

[1] Isaiah 50:4, Revised.

country district, where the crowds which the village could not hold now throng about Him. Now note what the Master does. The authorized version says, "He withdrew into the wilderness and prayed." A more nearly literal reading would be, "He was retiring in the deserts and praying"; suggesting not a single act, but rather *a habit of action* running through several days or even weeks. That is, being compelled by the greatness of the crowds to go into the deserts or country districts, and being constantly thronged there by the people, He had *less opportunity* to get alone, and yet more need, and so while He patiently continues His work among them He studiously seeks opportunity to retire at intervals from the crowds to pray.

How much His life was like ours. Pressed by duties, by opportunities for service, by the great need around us, we are strongly tempted to give less time to the inner chamber, with door shut "Surely this work must be done," we think, "though it does crowd and flurry our prayer time some." *"No,"* the Master's practice here says with intense emphasis. Not work first, and prayer to bless it. But the *first* place given to prayer and then the service growing out of such prayer will be charged with unmeasured power. The greater the outer pressure on His closet-life, the more jealously He guarded against either a shortening of its time or a flurrying of its spirit. The tighter the tension, the more time must there be for unhurried prayer.

The fourth mention is found in Luke, chapter six. "It came to pass in these days that He went out into the mountains to pray, and He continued all night in prayer to God." The time is probably about the middle of the second year of His public ministry. He had been having very exasperating experiences with the national leaders from Judea who dogged His steps, criticising and nagging at every turn, sowing seeds of skepticism among His simple-minded, intense-spirited Galileans. It was also the day *before* He selected the twelve men who were to be the leaders after His departure, and preached the mountain sermon. Luke does not say that He *planned* to spend the entire night in prayer. Wearied in spirit by the ceaseless petty picking and Satanic hatred of His enemies, thinking of the serious work of the morrow, there was just one thing for Him to do. He knew where to find rest, and sweet fellowship, and a calming presence, and wise counsel. Turning His face northward He sought the solitude of the mountain not far off for quiet meditation and prayer. And as He prayed and listened and talked without words, daylight gradually grew into twilight, and that yielded imperceptibly to the brilliant Oriental stars spraying down their lustrous fire-light. And still He prayed, while the darkness below and the blue above deepened, and the stilling calm of God wrapped all nature around, and hushed His heart into a deeper peace. In the fascination of the Father's loving presence He was utterly lost to the flight of time, but prayed on and on until, by and by, the earth had once more completed its daily turn, the gray streaks of dawnlight crept up the east, and the face of Palestine, fragrant with the deep dews of an eastern night, was kissed by a sun of a new day. And then, "when it was day"—how quietly the narrative goes on—"He called the disciples and *chose* from them twelve,—and a great multitude of disciples and of the people came,—and He *healed* all—and He opened His mouth and *taught* them—*for power came forth from Him.*" Is it any wonder, after such a night! If all our exasperations and embarrassments were followed, and all our decisions and utterances preceded, by unhurried prayer, what power would come forth from us, too. Because as He is even so are we in this world.

The fifth mention is made by Matthew, chapter fourteen, and Mark, chapter six, John hinting at it in chapter six of his gospel. It was about the time of the third passover, the beginning of His last year of service. Both He and the disciples had been kept exceedingly busy with the great throng coming and

going incessantly. The startling news had just come of the
tragic death of His forerunner. There was need of bodily rest,
as well as of quiet to think over the rapidly culminating opposition. So taking boat they headed towards the eastern
shore of the lake. But the eager crowds watched the direction
taken and spreading the news, literally "ran" around the
head of the lake and ¢"out-went them," and when He stepped
from the boat for the much-needed rest there was an immense
company, numbering thousands, waiting for Him. Did some
feeling of impatience break out among the disciples that they
could not be allowed a little leisure? Very likely, for they were
so much like us. But *He* was "moved with compassion" and,
wearied though He was, patiently spent the entire day in
teaching, and then, at eventime when the disciples proposed
sending them away for food, He, with a handful of loaves
and fishes, satisfied the bodily cravings of as many as five
thousand.

There is nothing that has so appealed to the masses in all
countries and all centuries as ability to furnish plenty to eat.
Literally tens of thousands of the human race fall asleep
every night hungry. So here. At once it is proposed by a great
popular uprising, under the leadership of this wonderful man
as king, to throw off the oppressive Roman yoke. Certainly if
only His consent could be had it would be immensely successful, they thought. Does this not rank with Satan's suggestion in the wilderness, and with the later possibility coming
through the visit of the Greek deputation, of establishing the
kingdom without suffering? It was a temptation, even though
it found no response within Him. With the overawing power
of His presence so markedly felt at times He quieted the
movement, "constrained"[1] the disciples to go by boat before
Him to the other side while He dismissed the throng.

---

[1]Does not this very strong language suggest that possibly the disiples had been
conferred with by the revolutionary leaders?

"And after He had *taken leave of them*"—what gentle courtesy and tenderness mingled with His irrevocable decision—"He went up in the mountain *to pray,*" and *"continued in prayer"* until the morning watch. A second night spent in prayer! Bodily weary, His spirit startled by an event which vividly foreshadowed His own approaching violent death, and now his vigorous renewal of His old temptation, again He had recourse to His one unfailing habit of getting off alone *to pray.* Time alone *to pray; more* time to pray, was His one invariable offset to all difficulties, all temptations, and all needs. How much more there must have been in prayer as He understood and practiced in than many of His disciples to-day know.

Deepening Shadows.

We shall perhaps understand better some of the remaining prayer incidents if we remember that Jesus is now in the last year of His ministry, the acute state of His experiences with the national leaders preceding the final break. The awful shadow of the cross grows deeper and darker across His path. The hatred of the opposition leader gets constantly intenser. The conditions of discipleship are more sharply put. The inability of the crowds, of the disciples, and others to understand Him grows more marked. Many followers go back. He seeks to get more time for intercourse with the twelve. He makes frequent trips to distant points on the border of the outside, non-Jewish world. The coming scenes and experiences—*the* scene on the little hillock outside the Jerusalem wall—seem never absent from His thoughts.

The sixth mention is made by Luke, chapter nine. They are up north in the neighbourhood of the Roman city of Caesarea Philippi. "And it came to pass as He was praying alone, the disciples were with Him." Alone, so far as the multitudes are concerned, but seeming to be drawing these twelve nearer to His inner life. Some of these later incidents seem to suggest that he was trying to woo them into something of the same love for the fascination of secret prayer that He had. How much they would need to pray in the coming years when He was gone. Possibly, too, He yearned for a closer fellowship with them. He loved human fellowship, as Peter and James and John, and Mary and Martha and many other gentle women well knew. And there is no fellowship among men to be compared with fellowship *in prayer.*

> "There is a place where *spirits blend,*
> *Where friend holds fellowship with friend,*
> A place than all beside more sweet,
> It is the blood-bought mercy-seat."

The seventh mention is in this same ninth chapter of Luke, and records a third night of prayer. Matthew and Mark also tell of the transfiguration scene, but it is Luke who explains that He went up into the mountain *to pray,* and that it was *as He was praying* that the fashion of His countenance was altered. Without stopping to study the purpose of this marvellous manisfestation of His divine glory to the chosen three at a time when desertion and hatred were so marked, it is enough now to note the significant fact that it was while *He was praying* that the wondrous change came. *Transfigured while praying!* And by His side stood one who centuries before on the earth had spent so much time alone with God that the glory-light of that presence transfigured *his* face, though he was unconscious of it. A shining face caused by contact with God! Shall not we, to whom the Master has said, "follow Me," get alone with Him and His blessed Word, so habitually, with open or uncovered face, that is, with eyesight unhindered by prejudice or self-seeking, that mirroring the glory of His face we shall more and more come to bear His very likeness upon our faces?[1]

[1] 2 Cor. 3:18

"And the face shines bright
    With a glow of light
    From His presence sent
    Whom she loves to meet.

"Yes, the face beams bright
    With an inner light
    As by day so by night,
    In shade as in shine,
    With a beauty fine,
    That she wist not of,
    From some source within,
        And above.

"Still the face shines bright
    With the glory-light
    From the mountain height,
    Where the resplendent sight
    Of His face
    Fills her view
    And illumines in turn
    First the few,
    Then the wide race."

The eighth mention is in the tenth chapter of Luke. He had organized a band of men, sending them out in two's into the places he expected to visit. They had returned with a joyful report of the power attending their work; and standing in their midst, His own heart overflowing with joy, He looked up and, as though the Father's face was visible, spake out to Him the gladness of His heart. He seemed to be always conscious of His Father's presence, and the most natural thing was to speak to Him. They were always within speaking distance of each other, and always on speaking terms.

The ninth mention is in the eleventh chapter of Luke, very

similar to the sixth mention, "It came to pass as He was praying in a certain place that when He ceased one of His disciples
said unto Him, 'Lord, teach us to pray.' " Without doubt
these disciples were praying men. He had already talked to
them a great deal about prayer. But as they noticed how large
a place prayer had in His life, and some of the marvellous
results, the fact came home to them with great force that
there must be some fascination, some power, some secret in
prayer, of which *they were ignorant*. This Man was a master
in the fine art of praying. *They* really did not know how to
pray, they thought. How their request must have delighted
Him! At last they were being aroused concerning *the* great
secret of power. May it be that this simple recital of His
habits of prayer may move every one of us to get alone with
Him and make the same earnest request. For the first step in
learning to pray is to pray,—"Lord, teach me to pray." And
who *can* teach like Him?

The tenth mention is found in John, chapter eleven, and is
the second of the four instances of ejaculatory prayer. A
large company is gathered outside the village of Bethany,
around a tomb in which four days before the body of a young
man had been laid away. There is Mary, still weeping, and
Martha, always keenly alive to the properties, trying to be
more composed, and their personal friends, and the villagers,
and the company of acquaintances and others from
Jerusalem. At His word, after some hesitation, the stone at
the mouth of the tomb is rolled aside. And Jesus lifted up His
eyes and said, "Father, I thank Thee that Thou heardest Me;
and I knew that Thou hearest Me always; but because of the
multitude that standeth around I said it that they may believe
that Thou didst send Me!" Clearly before coming to the tomb
He had been praying in secret about the raising of Lazarus,
and what followed was in answer to His prayer. How plain it
becomes that all the marvellous power displayed in His brief
earthly career *came through prayer*. What inseparable inti-

macy between His life of activity at which the multitude then and ever since has marvelled, and His hidden closet-life of which only these passing glimpses are obtained. Surely the greatest power entrusted to man is prayer-power. But how many of us are untrue to the trust, while this strangely omnipotent power put into our hands lies so largely unused.

Note also the certainty of His faith in the Hearer of prayer: "I thank Thee that Thou heardest Me." There was nothing that could be *seen* to warrant such faith. There lay the dead body. But He trusted as *seeing* Him who is *invisible*. Faith is blind, except upward. It is blind to impossibilities and deaf to doubt. It listens only to God and sees only His power and acts accordingly. Faith is not believing that He *can* but that He *will*. But such faith comes only of close continuous contact with God. Its birthplace is in the secret closet; and time and the open Word, and an awakened ear and a reverent quiet heart are necessary to its growth.

The eleventh mention is found in the twelfth chapter of John. Two or three days before the fated Friday some Greek visitors to the Jewish feast of Passover sought an interview with Him. The request seemed to bring to His mind a vision of the great outside world, after which His heart yearned, coming to Him so hungry for what only He could give. And instantly athwart that vision like an ink-black shadow came the other vision, never absent now from His waking thoughts, *of the cross* so awfully near. Shrinking in horror from the second vision, yet knowing that only through its realization could be realized the first,—seemingly forgetful for the moment of the bystanders, as though soliloquizing, He speaks—"now is My soul troubled; and what shall I say? Shall I say, Father *save* Me from this hour? But for this cause came I unto this hour: *this* is what I will say (and the intense conflict of soul merges into the complete victory of a wholly surrendered will) *Father, glorify Thy name.*" Quick as the prayer was uttered, came the audible voice out of heaven

answering, "I have both glorified it and will glorify it again."
How near heaven must be! How quickly the Father hears! He
must be bending over, intently listening, eager to catch even
faintly whispered prayer. Their ears, full of earth-sounds,
unaccustomed to listening to a heavenly voice, could hear
nothing intelligible. He had a *trained ear*. Isaiah 50:4 revised
(a passage plainly prophetic of Him), suggests how it was that
He could understand this voice so easily and quickly. "He
wakeneth morning by morning, He wakeneth mine ear to
hear as they that are taught." A taught ear is as necessary to
prayer as a taught tongue, and the daily morning appointment with God seems essential to both.

Under the Olive Trees.

The twelfth mention is made by Luke, chapter twenty-two.
It is Thursday night of Passion week, in the large upper room
in Jerusalem where He is celebrating the old Passover feast,
and initiating the new memorial feast. But even that hallowed
hour is disturbed by the disciples' self-seeking disputes. With
the great patience of great love He gives them the wonderful
example of humility of which John thirteen tells, speaking
gently of what it meant, and then turning to Peter, and using
his old name, He says, "Simon, Simon, behold Satan asked
to have you that he might sift you as wheat, but I made supplication for thee that thy faith fail not." *He had been praying for Peter by name!* That was one of His prayer-habits,
praying for others. And He has not broken off that blessed
habit yet. He is able to save to the uttermost them that draw
near to God through Him *seeing He ever liveth to make in-
tercesion for them*. His occupation now seated at His
Father's right hand in glory is *praying for each of us* who
trust Him. By name? Why not?

The thirteenth mention is the familiar one in John, chapter
seventeen, and cannot be studied within these narrow limits,
but merely fitted into its order. The twelfth chapter contains

His last words to the world. In the thirteenth and through to the close of this seventeenth He is alone with His disciples. If this prayer is read carefully in the revised version it will be seen that its standpoint is that of one who thinks of His work down in the world as already done (though the chief scene is yet to come) and the world left behind, and now He is about re-entering His Father's presence to be re-instanted in glory there. It is really, therefore, a sort of specimen of the praying for us in which He is *now* engaged, and so is commonly called the intercessory of high-priestly prayer. For thirty years He lived a perfect life. For three and a half years He was a prophet speaking to men for God. For nineteen centuries He has been high priest speaking to God for men. When He returns it will be as King to reign over men for God.

The fourteenth mention brings us within the sadly sacred precincts of Gethsemane garden, one of His favourite prayer-spots, where He frequently went while in Jerusalem. The record is found in Matthew twenty-six, Mark fourteen, and Luke twenty-one. Let us approach with hearts hushed and heads bared and bowed, for this is indeed hallowed ground. It is a little later on that same Thursday night, into which so much has already been pressed and so much more is yet to come. After the talk in the upper room, and the simple wondrous prayer, He leads the little band out of the city gate on the east across the swift, muddy Kidron into the inclosed grove of olive trees beyond. There would be no sleep for Him that night. Within an hour or two the Roman soldiers and the Jewish mob, led by the traitor, will be there searching for Him, and He meant to spend the intervening time in *prayer*. With the longing for sympathy so marked during these latter months, He takes Peter and James and John and goes farther into the deeply-shadowed grove. But now some invisible power tears him away and plunges Him alone still farther into the moonlit recesses of the garden; and there is a strange, awful struggle of soul ensues. It seems like a renewal of the same conflict He experienced in John twelve when the Greeks came, but immeasurably intenser. He who in Himself knew no sin was now beginning to realize in His spirit what within a few hours He realized *actually,* that He was in very deed to be made sin for us. And the awful realization comes in upon Him with such terrific intensity that it seems as though His physical frame cannot endure the strain of mental agony. The *actual* experience of the next day produced such mental agony that His physical strength gave way. For He died not of His physical suffering, excruciating as that was, but literally of a broken heart, its walls burst asunder by the strain of soul. It is not possible for a sinning soul to appreciate with what nightmare dread and horror the sinless soul of Jesus must have approached the coming contact with the sin of a world. With bated breath and reverent gaze one follows that lonely figure among the trees; now kneeling, now falling upon His face, lying postrate, "He prayed that *if* it were possible the hour might pass away from Him." One snatch of that prayer reaches our ears: "Abba, Father, all things are possible unto Thee—*if* it be possible let this cup pass away from Me; nevertheless not as I will, but as Thou wilt." How long He remained so in prayer we do not know, but so great was the tension of spirit that a messenger from heaven appeared and strengthened Him. Even after that "being in an agony He prayed more earnestly (literally, more stretched out, more strainedly) and His sweat became as it were great clots of blood falling down upon the ground." When at length He arises from that season of conflict and prayer, the victory seems to be won, and something of the old-time calm reasserts itself. He goes to the sleeping disciples, and mindful of their coming temptation, admonishes them to pray; then returns to the lonely solitude again for more prayer, but the change in the form of prayer tells of the triumph of soul, "O My Father, if this cup *cannot* pass away except I drink it, Thy will be done." The victory is complete. The crisis is past. He yields Himself to that dreaded experience through which alone the Father's loving plan for a dying world can be accomplished. Again He returns to the poor, weak disciples, and back again for another bit of strengthening communion, and then the flickering glare of torches in the distance tells Him that "the hour is come." With steady step and a marvellous peace lighting His face He goes out to meet His enemies. He overcame in this greatest crisis of His life *by prayer*.

The fifteenth mention is the final one. Of the seven sentences which He spake upon the cross, three were prayers. Luke tells us that while the soldiers were driving the nails through His hands and feet and lifting the cross into place, He, thinking even then not of self, but of others, said, "Father, forgive them, they know not what they do."

It was as the time of the daily evening sacrifice drew on, near the close of that strange darkness which overcast all nature, after a silence of three hours, that He loudly sobbed out the piercing, heart-rendering cry, "My God, My God, why didst Thou forsake Me?" A little later the triumphant shout proclaimed His work done, and then the very last word was a prayer quietly breathed out, as He yielded up His life, "Father, into Thy hands I commend My spirit." And so His expiring breath was vocalized into prayer.

A Composite Picture.

It may be helpful to make the following summary of these allusions.

1. *His times of prayer:* His regular habit seems plainly to have been to devote the early morning hour to communion with His Father, and to depend upon that for constant guidance and instruction. This is suggested especially by Mark 1:35; and also by Isaiah 50:4-6 coupled with John 7:16 l.c., 8:28, and 12:49.

In addition to this regular appointment He sought other

opportunities for secret prayer as special need arose; late at night after others had retired; three times He remained in prayer all the night; and at irregular intervals between times. Note that it was usually a *quiet* time when the noises of earth were hushed. He spent special time in prayer *before* important events and also *afterwards*. (See mentions 1, 2, 3, 4, 5, 10 and 14.)

2. *His places of prayer:* He who said, "Enter into thine inner chamber and when thou hast shut the door, pray to thy Father in secret," Himself had no fixed inner chamber, during His public career, to make easier the habitual retirement for prayer. Homeless for the three and a half years of ceaseless travelling, His place of prayer was a desert place, "the deserts," "the mountains," "a solitary place." He loved nature. The hilltop back of Nazareth village, the slopes of Olivet, the hillsides overlooking the Galilean lake, were His favourite places. Note that it was always a *quiet* place, shut away from the discordant sounds of earth.

3. *His constant spirit of prayer:* He was never out of the spirit of prayer. He could be alone in a dense crowd. It has been said that there are sorts of solitude, namely, of time, as early morning, or late at night; solitude of place, as a hilltop, or forest, or a secluded room; and solitude of spirit, as when one surrounded by a crowd may watch them unmoved, or to be lost to all around in his own inner thought. Jesus used all three sorts of solitude for talking with His Father. (See mentions 8, 10, 11 and 15.)

4. *He prayed in the great crises of His life:* Five such are mentioned: Before the awful battle royal with Satan in the Quarantanian wilderness at the outset; before choosing the twelve leaders of the new movement; at the time of the Galilean uprising; before the final departure from Galilee for Judea and Jerusalem; and in Gethsemane, the greatest crisis of all. (See mentions 1, 4, 5, 7 and 14.)

5. He prayed for others by name, and still does. (See

mention 13.)

6. *He prayed with others:* A habit that might well be more widely copied. A few minutes spent in quiet prayer by friends or fellow-workers before parting wonderfully sweetens the spirit, and cements friendships, and makes difficulties less difficult, and hard problems easier of solution. (See mentions 7, 9 and 13.)

7. *The greatest blessings of His life came during prayer:* Six incidents are noted: while praying, the Holy Spirit came upon Him; He was transfigured; three times a heavenly voice of approval came; and in His hour of sorest distress in the garden a heavenly messenger came to strengthen Him. (See mentions 1, 7, 11 and 14.)

How much prayer meant to Jesus! It was not only His *regular habit,* but His resort in *every emergency,* however slight or serious. When perplexed He *prayed.* When hard pressed by work He *prayed.* When hungry for fellowship He found it in *prayer.* He chose His associates and received His messages *upon His knees.* If tempted, He *prayed.* If criticised, He *prayed.* If fatigued in body or wearied in spirit, He had recourse to His one unfailing habit of *prayer. Prayer* brought Him *unmeasured power* at the beginning, and *kept* the flow unbroken and undiminished. There was no emergency, no difficulty, no necessity, no temptation that would not yield to prayer, as He practiced it. Shall not we, who have been tracing these steps in His prayer-life, go back over them again and again until we breathe in His very spirit of prayer? And shall we not, ask Him daily to teach us how to pray, and then plan to get alone with Him regularly and He may have opportunity to teach us, and we the opportunity to practice His teaching?